Beginning Zen

A Source Book for
the Spiritual Path

Beginning Zen

A Source Book for
the Spiritual Path

Maria Kannon Zen Center
1998

The Maria Kannon Zen Center provides a setting for Zen practice in Dallas, Texas under the direction of Ruben Habito, an authorized teacher in the Sanbô Kyôdan lineage of Kamakura, Japan. MKZC is a lay tradition and is open to everyone without restriction.

ISBN 0-9663245-0-1

Maria Kannon Zen Center
P.O. Box 270441, Dallas TX 75227-0441
6532 Hunnicut Road, Dallas, TX 75227
Tel: 214-388-1122   Email: ti_sarana@yahoo.com
http://www.mkzc.org

Dedication

to Maria Kannon

Table of Contents

Table of Contents

Part II - The Lineage

Preface

This book is an invitation to a spiritual path. Its basic message is "taste and see!" Material is presented on the basics of developing and nurturing Zen practice in a Western cultural setting—the why, what, and how.

For more detailed treatment, especially recommended are Ruben Habito's two books, *Total Liberation: Zen Spirituality and the Social Dimension* and *Healing Breath: Zen Spirituality for a Wounded Earth*, both published by Orbis Books. Also recommended is *The Three Pillars of Zen* (Boston: Beacon Press, 1965), edited by Philip Kapleau, a collection based on the Zen practice and teaching of Sanbô Kyôdan tradition that began in Kamakura, Japan.

I have drawn on many existing books and other reference sources in my attempt to aid those who wish to practice Zen and intgrate it in their daily life.

Gratitude is owed to Mr. Stephen Taylor, Mr. Chris Schirber, and the Board of Directors of the Trust for the Meditation Process based in St. Paul, Minnesota, whose generous assistance enabled this manual to be published.

Special thanks go to the MKZC Board of Directors for their patience and encouragement in the production of this book; to Tom Ottinger for cover design, to Helen Cortes and Skip Nall for the photographs of zazen postures, and Jim Crump for the Texas Oxherding illustrations; to Dr. T. Matthew Ciolek of Canberra, Australia, for permission to reproduce some of his excellent Sanbô Kyôdan resources from his World Wide Web pages; to Katherine Robertson for layout, design, production, and "encouragement"; to Bob Curry for seeing through the details toward the publication of this volume; and to the Maria Kannon Zen Center community, for just being.

Rex Robertson

Part I

The Practice

1 What is Zen?

> The unexamined life
> is not worth living
> *- Socrates*
>
> Thoroughly to know oneself,
> is above all art,
> for it is the highest art
> *- Theologica Germanica*
>
> Thou shalt know God
> without image
> and without means
> *- Meister Eckhart*
>
> Eat this, and drink tea
> *- Sengai*

Zen?

Zen is awakening to the dynamic reality of the present moment. The practice of Zen is life itself, embodying radical inquiry into the true nature of the Self and of the true nature of reality. To practice Zen meditation is in itself an expression of this reality, an embodiment of the awakened state.

The term "Zen" is the Japanese pronunciation of the Chinese term *Ch'an*, which in turn derives from the Sanskrit term *Dhyâna*. Dhyâna can be translated as "meditation," "absorption of mind," or "fullness of attention."

Zen Practice

The formal practice of Zen meditation is called *zazen*, which literally means "sitting Zen." However, the practice of zazen is not meditation or contemplation, as these terms are commonly understood in the West. Nor is the practice of Zen limited only to periods of sitting in the formal postures of meditation. True Zen is actualized in every moment of being; in the fullness of the moment, the awareness of the breath, in the midst of all activities, even extending into sleep.

Zazen involves a process that develops a centered, focused awareness, integrating body and mind into the heart of life itself. In zazen, the body is placed in a meditative posture of dynamic relaxation; the natural, relaxed flow of the breath is experienced fully. The mind is brought to full awareness in the present moment, the here and now.

Zen practice grew from the initial experience of the enlightenment or awakening of the historical Buddha Gautama Shâkyamuni and the fertile ground of Buddhism as it developed in China and Japan. With the introduction of Zen to Europe and the Americas, much thought, study and experimentation is underway in the development of Zen practice that is not necessarily "Buddhist" in the sectarian sense of the term.

Much of this ground breaking work has been developed by the Sanbô Kyôdan (Three Treasures) tradition, which seeks not only to unite the best aspects of the Rinzai and Sôtô Zen lineages, but to open Zen practice to persons of non-Buddhist backgrounds and to those who claim no particular religious observation (Chapter 14, *is Zen a Religion?* and Chapter 15, *Zen Practice and Christians*). This approach has been underway for over forty years and is bearing fruit in the lives of many people.

Zen has been called the "religion before religion" or "the heart of religion." In this sense, Zen is a radical approach to Truth. Zen is non-religious, non-conceptual, non-theoretical, non-theological. Zen is an extremely radical and practical approach to spirituality, developed and refined over the centuries and drawing on the rich traditions of India, China and Japan. In many ways, Zen can be called a mysticism of the ordinary.

Zen has had a tremendous impact in the culture of Japan, influencing art, literature, drama, architecture, and the martial arts, to name but a few aspects. The effect of Zen on Western culture, and of Western culture on Zen, is an ongoing experiment in which you are invited to participate.

Zen is radical in the sense that the ultimate authority is one's own personal experience of Reality, as guided by a recognized teacher. This unique approach to awakening is best characterized by the "Four Marks of Zen," attributed to the first Zen Patriarch, Bodhidharma:

- A special transmission outside the scriptures
- No dependence on words or letters
- Direct pointing to the human mind and heart
- Seeing into one's true nature

In Zen practice, one takes nothing for granted, questions everything. All teachings, all concepts, all beliefs, all truths, even all experiences are to be doubted and questioned.

You are invited to experience the heart of your being and to participate consciously in the unfolding and shaping of the universe, in the depths and dynamism of the present moment.

> But then if I do not strive, who will?
> - *Chuang Tzu*

> No striving, no attainment. No one strives,
> there is nothing to attain.
> - *anonymous Zen monk*

2 Why Practice?

The Four Fundamental Aspirations

The desire to enter into Zen practice can usually be placed in one of four broad aspirations, as outlined below.

Simple Curiosity

The first aspiration or desire to study Zen is simple curiosity: What is Zen, and what is it about? Perhaps you have read various philosophies, and you desire to see what is unique about Zen. Or perhaps you have encountered Zen ink paintings or poetry, or seen pictures of Zen temples and gardens, and wonder what inspires such an artistic expression. In any event, you simply want to see what Zen is all about.

The Desire for Physical Well-being

The second aspiration for exploring Zen is the desire to experience improvements in physical well being. Meditation has been well documented as a proven means of deep relaxation and stress management, and Zen offers a particular way to experience this in your life. Zen meditation can be a positive factor toward the healing of ailments, such as cancer, heart disease, and nervous disorders.

The Desire to Travel a Spiritual Path

The third aspiration to explore the practice of Zen is the desire to travel a spiritual path, to find inner peace.

In this society, we are constantly deluged by images of materialism and violence. Perhaps you desire to experience a sense of being centered, of being at peace with yourself in the midst of the chaos of contemporary life. Zen practice can be seen as offering this experience.

"Having One's Hair Aflame"

The fourth aspiration to practice Zen would be the desire to resolve the fundamental questions of one's existence, the questions of life and death, of one's place in the universe: Who or what am I? Where did I come from? Where am I going? What does all this really mean? In Zen terminology, this is the desire to awaken to one's true self or true nature, not in an intellectual manner, but through firsthand experience. This aspiration can become an overwhelming obsession, and is sometimes known as "having one's hair aflame."

These fundamental aspirations represent a summary of the basic reasons one may desire to practice Zen. All approaches are equally valid as starting points. All aspirations can be purified and can then lead to a deep spirituality, but the third and fourth aspirations described above dispose one to receive the rich treasures that Zen practice can open in one's life.

3 Approaching Practice

Does One Have Buddha Nature?

In Zen, one's true self or true nature is referred to as "Buddha nature." The term "Buddha" simply means "awakened one," and so Buddha nature simply points to the fact that you are inherently enlightened, already awake. But just as there are different levels of wakefulness, you can deepen your awareness in the practice of Zen.

The analogy of water is often used to illustrate this point. Water exists in three physical states; as a solid in ice, as a flowing liquid, and as an invisible vapor in steam or clouds. In each state, whether that of ice, liquid, or vapor, the fundamental nature of water is unchanging; that is, every expression of water, on the molecular level, is always comprised of two atoms of hydrogen and one atom of oxygen.

To extend the analogy to the human condition, in much the same way, the conscious but unawakened mind is like ice, with rigid thought, perceptual, belief, emotional, and experiential patterns. The awakening mind becomes like water, liquid and flowing, unconfined. The enlightened or fully awakened mind is like vapor, unbounded, limitless, empty, clear.

In our normal experience, ice will melt and begin to flow in the liquid state, and then as liquid, will eventually vaporize. So too does mind aspire to Mind.

Awakening to one's true nature is a natural expression of becoming fully human. With this in mind, there are several fundamental attitudes that will aid in developing your practice.

Fundamental Attitudes

Three fundamental attitudes are recommended for you to keep in mind when undertaking Zen practice. These attitudes are great trust or faith; great doubt; and great persistence or perserverance.

Great Trust

Great trust or great faith is a presupposition in the practice of Zen. This is not to confuse faith with belief; Zen requires no particular belief as a prerequisite to practice. Indeed, certain beliefs or opinions might actually hinder practice.

Great trust, rather, is placed in the tradition of Zen practice. This trust includes an acceptance of the invitation to experience your true self as awakened. This faith or trust is accompanied by the certitude that there is deep value in the practice of Zen, that the living tradition of over 2,500 years of Zen practice can make an immense difference in one's life.

The practice of zazen is also an expression of trust in a "fundamental sanity" in the midst of a chaotic world. Face to face with the reality of impermanence, Zen is total immersion in the eternal now, the changeless yet ever changing moment.

Great Doubt

The other side of, and complement to great trust, is great doubt. Doubt is required for the serious inquiry into the nature of reality, into the nature of the self, as actualized in the practice of Zen. Doubt is not to be understood as negativity. Rather, doubt expresses itself in the fundamental questions that you bring to your practice of Zen.

Doubt is the spirit of questioning you bring to your practice. "Who am I, really? What is this really all about?" Doubt in this sense is the ability to remain completely open, a willingness to question assumptions, experiences, beliefs, opinions. Doubt is the continuous questioning of your own existence, and of questioning your insights—and the insights, teachings and experience of others. Truth is often likened to a sword, or a stylized thunderbolt, that cuts away and penetrates ALL illusions. Doubt is the cutting edge of the sword of truth.

Great doubt accompanies an attitude of openness, of acceptance. It is a willingness to question everything, and a willingness to live with the possibility that the questions may never be answered.

Great Persistence

The third attitude fundamental to Zen practice is great persistence or perserverance. The commitment to perservering is the foundation of mature practice, beyond the considerations of personal growth, attainment, or awakening; beyond the times of realization and insight, beyond the times of difficulties, doubts or other weaknesses.

Your practice IS the manifestation of your enlightenment; your practice IS your life. The practice of Zen is not confined to formal sitting. Practice is not separate from life, one's particular situation or circumstances. One develops the ability to practice in all situations and circumstances.

Zen tends to strip excuses, the "if only's" out of your life; if only I had time to practice; if only I had a place to practice; if only my butt didn't hurt. . . Your life is your practice, and your commitment to developing your practice is the commitment to the quality of your life.

The practice of Zen leads to an acceptance of total responsibility for the character and expression of your life.

What Happens in Zen Practice

With persistence in zazen, you will begin to realize the fruits of practice. It is important to recognize that the fruits of practice are a by-product of continued and committed practice, not ends to be sought in themselves. As you continue zazen on a regular basis, you will notice an increase in vitality and energy, and a deepening awareness of events and situations around you, as well as increased awareness of your internal world of thoughts, emotions, and physical sensations.

The regular periods of stillness, of relaxation, of concentrated breathing, all contribute to improved health. To still the body is to still the mind, and vice-versa. A quiet and centered body-mind realizes and begins to release the amount of tension and stress carried in muscles and thought. This realization leads to a deepening acceptance of reality, a letting go of pain, pressures, tensions, obstacles.

Focus on the breath, besides stilling the mind, expands into the ability to center one's being in daily life. You may notice an increased ability to concentrate on whatever task is at hand, to pay closer attention to details, to listen better.

Regular zazen also brings a sense of detachment or distance from the craziness of daily life and from the tumult of the undisciplined mind and the passions of sensory input. The normal conscious mind is sometimes likened to a runaway chariot, pulled headlong by the five horses of the senses. You begin to realize that much of the insanity perceived in the world "out there" is in reality the tempestuous fluctuations of your own chaotic thoughts.

Detachment or distancing does not mean removal or retreat from the world; on the contrary, this practice brings a greater engagement with the world, but on a different and more effective level. You can truly observe the workings of situations, the dynamics of personalities and emotions at play, and can contribute to restoring balance in a real, rather than emotional sense, as you become aware of your connectedness with the world at a deeper level.

As you see through the ego and its machinations, you are free to act consciously in a manner that is particularly appropriate to the current situation, rather than being limited to unconscious reactions. This freedom allows a condition of spontaneous and continuous creativity in all situations, a sense of the truly open mind, capable of extreme fluidity and flexibility in thought and attitude; you can flow like water. There is no ego to support, no need to be right, no territory to defend. There is only the situation in the moment, with all the richness, complexity and wonder.

With continued regular zazen, you are likely to experience different levels of insight or realization. Answers to particular questions might suddenly be answered, or unsolvable dilemmas might be resolved. This is properly a topic only for consultation with the teacher in a one-to-one encounter, so nothing further will be said here.

Unusual Phenomena

When beginning zazen, it is possible to experience illusions, visions, colors, physical sensations, etc. These phenomena are known as *makyô*, translated as "illusory state of mind."

Through deep meditation, it is possible that you might experience sensory phenomena, such as changes in the quality of perceived light or your eyesight; you might hear sound, such as voices or bells. You could smell pleasant (or unpleasant) scents. You might even feel physical sensations in various parts of the body. It is also possible that you might perceive very unsettling images or emotions, the opposite extreme of pleasant images and feelings.

These experiences can be understood as signals from the subconscious realm. Any experience of this kind should be discussed with the teacher. These experiences can be the result of intensifying practice, or can be caused by the freeing up of accumulated psychic, mental or emotional debris, or even the release of physical tension.

These experiences may be indications of your personal deepening sense of zazen, but they have no particular value in themselves, and are neither to be sought after or feared. You should simply observe, suspending both judgement and involvement, and continue with practice.

4   Fruits of the Zen Life

Fruits of the Zen Life

What happens in your life as you engage in Zen practice? There are three fruits that manifest themselves in the life of the practicioner. These are:

- The centering of one's being
- The experience of awakening
- The embodiment of awakening in one's daily life

Centering Your Being

The Japanese term for the first fruit of Zen practice is *jôriki*, which can literally be translated as "the power of *samâdhi*." The latter is a Sanskrit word which refers to a unitive state of awareness, wherein the subject-object polarity is overcome, and everything is seen in clear light "just as it is."

We can describe this state of awareness, which goes on deepening with regular Zen practice, as leading to a centering of your being, toward a deeper sense of integration.

As we live our lives in this phenomenal world, we find ourselves driven in various directions, dispersed in our interests and desires. Our lives are characterized by what the Buddha called *duhkha*, or "unsatisfactoriness." Literally *duhkha* is a compound from the word "wheel" (*kha*) and a prefix that is equivalent to the Latin-based "*mal*" (as in malpractice or malnutrition). The word dukkha thus signifies a state of being that is like a wheel that is misplaced, off-center, dislocated, and thus, dysfunctional. This is the state of being that we find ourselves in as we pursue various goals in life, as we let ourselves be driven by varios cravings and desires, as we let ourselves be dispersed in various directions, and find ourselves "dis-integrated."

Zen practice can enable us to see our situation more clearly, and also enable us to pick up the disparate pieces of our lives, leading us to become more centered and focused. We are thus gradually able to experience our lives moving in the direction of integration, toward a greater sense of wholeness.

The Experience of Awakening

As the first fruit described above continues to mature in the life of a practitioner, the ground becomes fertile for the appearance of the second fruit, which is the experience of awakening or enlightenment. The Japanese word for this is *kenshô*, literally "seeing one's true nature."

For some practitioners, this can come after a few weeks or a few months of practice, for others it may take years and years, depending on the "karmic baggage" each one carries. But whatever amount of time it takes, it is an experience that can definitively transform one's view of the world and of oneself.

What happens can be described as the falling away of the scales of one's eyes, in a way that one is now enabled to see "things as they really are," and no longer through one's subjective (ego) consciousness. To see things as they really are is also to see oneself "just as one is," that is, in a way no longer tainted by the perception of a delusive or deluded ego.

There are many published accounts of such experiences in Zen history, and a good number of *kôans* handed down in the Zen tradition are based on anecdotes of such enlightenment experiences (see Philip Kapleau, ed., *The Three Pillars of Zen,* for a collection of such accounts by twentieth-century practitioners).

The awakening experience can be precipitated by the habitual practice of Zen, with the gradual deepening or *samâdhi* or the first fruit of practice. It can also be evoked through practice with *kôans* under the direction of an authentic teacher who has been trained in helping others in nurturing this experience (see Chapter 5, *Fundamentals of Zazen*). It may happen in the context of an intensive Zen retreat (see Chapter 8, S*esshin*), or it may come totally unexpected and in a variety of contexts.

Yamada Kôun Rôshi's account serves as a notable example in this regard (excerpted from *The Three Pillars of Zen*, pp. 215-217).

"The day after I called on you I was riding home on the train with my wife. I was reading a book on Zen by Son-o, who, you may recall, was a master of Sôtô Zen living in Sendai during the Genroku period [1688-1703]. As the train was nearing Ofuna station I ran across this line: 'I came to realize clearly that Mind is no other than mountains and rivers and the great wide earth, the sun and the moon and the stars.'

"I had read this before, but this time it impressed itself upon me so vividly that I was startled. I said to myself: 'After seven or eight years of zazen I have finally perceived the essence of this statement,' and couldn't suppress the tears that began to well up. Somewhat ashamed to find myself crying among the crowd, I averted my face and dabbed at my eyes with my handkerchief.

"Meanwhile the train had arrived at Kamakura station and my wife and I got off. On the way home I said to her: 'In my present exhilarated frame of mind I could rise to the greatest heights.' Laughingly she replied: 'Then where would I be?' All the while I kept repeating that quotation to myself.

"It so happened that that day my younger brother and his wife were staying at my home, and I told them about my visit to your monastery and about that American who had come to Japan again only to attain enlightenment. In short, I told them all the stories you had told me, and it was after eleven thirty before I went to bed.

"At midnight I abruptly awakened. At first my mind was foggy, then suddenly that quotation flashed into my consciousness: 'I came to realize clearly that Mind is no other than mountains, rivers, and the great wide earth, the sun and the moon and the stars.' And I repeated it. Then all at once I was struck as though by lightning, and the next instant heaven and earth crumbled and disappeared. Instantaneously,

like surging waves, a tremendous delight welled up in me, a veritable hurricane of delight, as I laughed loudly and wildly: 'Ha, ha, ha, ha, ha, ha! There's no reasoning here, no reasoning at all! Ha, ha, ha!' The empty sky split in two, then opened its enormous mouth and began to laugh uproariously: 'Ha, ha, ha!' Later one of the members of my family told me that my laughter had sounded inhuman.

"I was now lying on my back. Suddenly I sat up and struck the bed with all my might and beat the floor with my feet, as if trying to smash it, all the while laughing riotously. My wife and youngest son, sleeping near me, were now awake and firghtened. Covering my mouth with her hand, my wife exlaimed: 'What's the matter with you? What's the matter with you?' But I wasn't aware of this until told about it afterwards. My son told me later he thought I had gone mad.

" 'I've come to enlightenment! Sâkyamuni and the patriarchs haven't deceived me! They haven't deceived me!' I remember crying out. When I calmed down I apologized to the rest of the family, who had come downstairs frightened by the commotion.

"Prostrating myself before the photograph of Kannon you had given me, the Diamond sûtra, and my volume of the book written by Yasutani-rôshi, I lit a stick of incense and did zazen until it was consumed half an hour later, thought it seemed only two or three minutes had elapsed.

"Even now my skin is quivering as I write.

"That morning I went to see Yasutani-rôshi and tried to decribe to him my experience of the sudden disintegration of heaven and earth. 'I am overjoyed, I am overjoyed!' I kept repeating, striking my thigh with vigor. Tears came which I couldn't stop. I tried to relate to him the experience of that night, but my mouth trembled and words wouldn't form themselves. In the end I just put my face in his lap. Patting me on the back he said: 'Well, well, it is rare indeed to experience to such a wonderful degree. It is termed "Attainment of the emptiness of Mind." You are to be congratulated!'

" 'Thanks to you,' I murmured, and again wept for joy. Repeatedly I told him: 'I must continue to apply myself energetically to zazen.' He was kind enough to give me detailed advice on how to pursue my practice in the future, after which he again whispered in my ear, 'My congratulations!' and escorted me to the foot of the mountain by flashlight.

"Although twenty-four hours have elapsed, I still feel the aftermath of that earthquake. My entire body is still shaking. I spent all of today laughing and weeping by myself.

"I am writing to report my experience in the hope that it will be of value to your monks, and because Yasutani-rôshi urged me to."

Embodiment in Daily Life

Different persons can experience awakening in varying degrees of intensity, and such an experience can totally transform one's way of seeing and one's way of relating to the world around. But such an experience is seen only as an initiation into the world of Zen.

Even without such an experience, an intelligent person may conceptually understand the truth of the interconnectedness of all beings, or the truth of emptiness. Or a practicioner may already be living a life grounded in wisdom and compassion to some extent. But what happens with the awakening experience is that these words such as "interconnectedness," or "emptiness," or "compassion" cease to be concepts, and become expressions of the reality that the practicioner begins to live, from moment to moment, in one's daily life.

The third fruit of Zen practice is the embodiment of the awakening experience in daily life, that is, the continual grounding of the practitioner in a life of wisdom and compassion. One deepens in the realization of interconnectedness in the different particularities it involves, as one deepens the experience of com-passion, that is, of suffering-with all sentient beings.

Continued practice after the awakening experience, especially with the aid of devices known as *kôans*, is a powerful way of assuring this deepening and of reconfirming the practicioner in this direction.

5 Fundamentals of Zazen

Modes of Practice

Zen includes all postures or possibilities of human activity and passivity, as follows:

- Zen in action (*gyôzen*)
- Zen in passivity or relaxation (*jûzen*)
- Seated Zen meditation (*zazen*)
- Zen in horizontal posture or sleep (*gazen*)

More information concerning these modes of Zen practice can be found in *Healing Breath: Zen Spirituality for a Wounded Earth*, pp. 38-57. The main point to remember is that practice is unceasing and not limited to formal periods of zazen.

Postures in Zazen

The heart of Zen practice is one's experience of reality, heightened through *zazen*, or seated meditation. In zazen practice, a correct posture is essential. "Correct" means observation of basic requirements that provide the foundation for an alert, dynamic, and relaxed state of being. The various postures are provided below for reference.

The basic postures of zazen include:

- Full lotus
- Half lotus
- Burmese position
- Kneeling position (with or without a bench)
- Sitting upright on a chair

The use of the *zafu* (pillow) and *zabuton* (mat) greatly facilitate the above positions. The zabuton provides a soft base that relieves pressure on the knees in the full or half lotus and Burmese positions. The zafu is designed to elevate the body, allowing for the slight rolling forward of the pelvis that helps keep the spine relaxed and erect. Extra cushions can be used to support the knees. A low bench is helpful for those who have difficulty in any of the cross-legged positions.

Full Lotus Position

The full lotus position (see Figure 5-1) is the traditional meditation pose used in most systems of yoga and meditation. It provides a very stable and balanced position that facilitates concentration and relaxation, while requiring little energy to maintain. This position may be difficult for people in the West to adopt.

Progress towards the full or half lotus position can be made by using stretching or limbering exercises for the legs and back, such as those found in hatha yoga. Even short periods of time spent in these positions will result in increased flexibility and the ability to maintain these postures for longer periods of time.

Figure 5-1, Full Lotus Position

Beginning Zen

To assume the full lotus position, take your seat on the zafu. Bend your legs, bringing the heels in to the zafu. Lift one foot with your hands, and place on the opposite thigh (it does not matter which leg is uppermost). The leg should be tucked tightly, but should also be relaxed, without excess pressure on either the ankles or thigh. The other leg then should be placed over the first leg, with the foot resting on the opposite thigh.

Ideally, the knees should rest on the zabuton; if one knee tends to "float" above the mat, more flexibility is required. The hands are brought together in the traditional position of meditation by placing them in the lap formed by the crossed legs, nested against the lower abdomen. The right hand serves as the base. The left hand is placed on top of the base hand, again with the palm up. The two thumbs are raised and the tips brought lightly together, forming a slight oval or circle. Do not press your thumbs together or let the circle collapse.

The tips of the thumbs are brought together gently, barely touching, to create a circle. No pressure should be felt on the thumbs. This position is a conscious gesture, requiring awareness to maintain. If you become drowsy or drift into daydreams, you will find the thumbs separating; gently closing the circle of the thumbs is a return to consciousness.

Keep your shoulders totally relaxed, but not slumped. Your arms can be brought forward slightly, pulled away from the body. This helps prevent tension in the shoulders.

Figure 5-2, Half Lotus Position

Half Lotus Position

To assume the half lotus position (see Figure 5-2), take your seat on the zafu. One leg is placed on the opposite thigh as in the full lotus position. The other leg is then pulled in, but instead of placing it on top of the leg, it is left on the zabuton. Both knees should be resting on the zabuton. The hands are arranged in the same position as in the full lotus.

Burmese Position

The Burmese position (see Figure 5-3) is similar to the full and half lotus, but easier on the knees and ankles. Seated on the zafu, both legs are bent and pulled inward. Neither foot is placed on the opposite thigh; the legs remain on the zabuton, but one foot is placed directly in front of the zafu. Both knees should lie flat on the zabuton. The hand position is the same as in the lotus positions.

Figure 5-3, Burmese Position

Kneeling Position

The kneeling position (see Figure 5-4) provides an alternative position to the cross-legged positions. To sit in this way, you can straddle the zafu; some people turn the zafu on end to add extra padding. The legs are folded in completely under the thighs; if you are positioned properly on the zafu, there will be very little pressure on your legs, knees and ankles.

As an alternative to the zafu, you can use a low bench. The bench provides a firmer base than the zafu. When using the bench, the legs are brought together and folded under the bench. The hands are placed in the lap in the same meditation position.

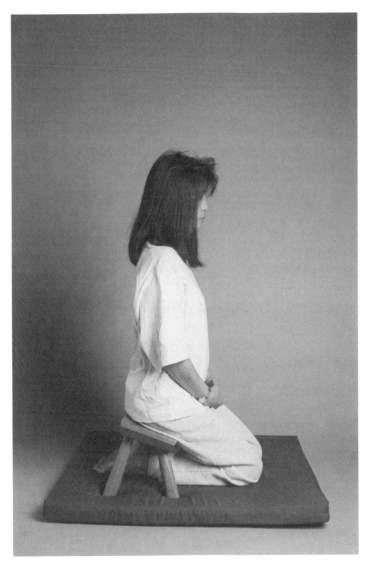

Figure 5-4, Kneeling Position

Zazen Using a Chair

If you cannot sit comfortably in any of the above positions, a chair is perfectly acceptable (see Figure 5-5). Again, all of the above considerations apply to sitting zazen in a chair, the exceptions being the legs. In this case, the feet should be flat on the floor. The knees should be approximately shoulder width apart. The hands are placed in the same meditation position.

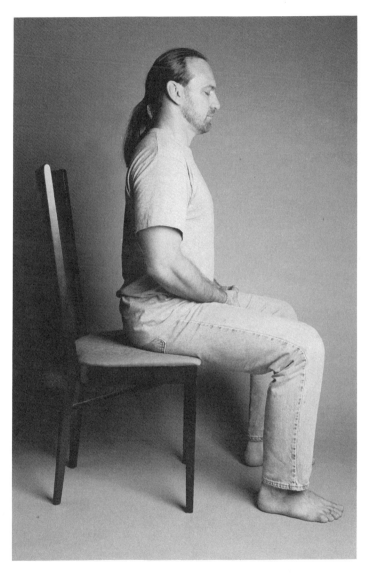

Figure 5-5, Chair Zazen

Other Considerations

You should work toward establishing a posture that can
be maintained for periods of from twenty to thirty minutes
without pain. If necessary, you can use additional small
cushions, placed beneath the zafu for height adjustments.
These can also be placed beneath knees that do not relax
completely to the zabuton.

Zazen can be practiced using any of the above postures;
however, there are some fundamental attitudes or
guidelines to keep in mind, no matter which meditation
posture you use.

Spine

In all postures, it is essential that the spine be kept erect.
The body should be in an attitude of relaxed alertness, or
dynamic stillness; military rigidity is inappropriate.
Therefore, you should experiment and choose a posture
that can be comfortably maintained for the duration of
the sitting period.

You can keep the spine relaxed and straight by mentally
imagining a straight line running through the spine,
entering through your head, down your erect spine.
Alternately, you can picture your vertebrae as beads on a
necklace, lightly suspended from above, or picture
yourself as serene as Mt. Fuji, firmly anchored on the
Earth, thoughts drifting like ethereal clouds in the vast
and empty sky.

When sitting in any of the cross-legged positions, the pelvis and abdomen should be rolled very slightly forward, accentuating the natural curvature of the spine. Be conscious not to let the pelvis slump backward; this will lead to lower back, neck, and shoulder pains, and fatigue.

Head

Your head can be perceived as if it is reaching effortlessly into the sky. Your head, neck and shoulders should be totally relaxed, with the head slightly tilted forward. The sense of the head reaching into the sky relieves tension in the neck and shoulders.

Be careful to relax your teeth and jaws, not to clench them. The upper and lower teeth should not be touching. You should place your tongue very gently against the back of the upper front teeth; this is a conscious gesture that relaxes the whole region of the mouth and jaw. The tongue should not press hard against the teeth, but very lightly float against them.

Eyes

The eyes should be half-open. Sit facing a wall to minimize external distractions. When facing a wall with the eyes partially open, the "flow" of external visual stimuli is reduced, so that visual distractions are minimized and the other senses are not aroused. If the eyes are totally closed, there is a tendency to drift into fantasies, daydreams or visualizations, or to fall asleep.

You should have the sense of letting your vision "flow" or "pour" into your being through the eyes. This is quite different than how we normally see, which is almost like grasping or clutching at objects of perception with our eyes. In some martial arts, this is known as "soft eyes," and develops keen peripheral vision, a focused center, and the ability to see through opponents' feints or other distractions.

In the beginning stages of zazen, you will find it helpful to sit facing a wall that is off-white or pastel in color, preferably with no heavy texture. It is not recommended to practice zazen facing a wall that is painted in primary or bright colors or vibrant patterns, such as is found in some wallpaper (i.e., stripes, twining vines, paisley, or cartoon characters). Soft, indirect lighting is recommended. Harsh or direct lighting creates glare and sharp visual contrasts that can be distracting; total darkness can lead to daydreaming or sleep.

Stillness

Absolute stillness in your chosen posture during zazen is essential. Body and mind are not two, so to still the body is to quiet the mind. Likewise, as the turbulence of everyday thought diminishes, the body settles into comfortable relaxation.

You can picture your meditation posture as a mountain of solemn majesty and proportion. Picture your crossed legs and meditation cushion as the base of the mountain, firmly rooted in the earth. Picture your body, as the body of the mountain, perfectly centered. Picture your head as the snow-covered peak "holding up the sky." Emotions and thoughts can be viewed as the flight of the winds, the gathering and passing of ephemereal clouds, or perhaps even the tumult of a thunderstorm; but in the midst of all these occurences, the mountain remains impervious; unmoved, undisturbed, serene and tranquil.

Breathing

Counting the breath is a basic exercise when beginning zazen, and develops focus, attention, and an alert, relaxed state. The breath is centered and drawn from the point just below the navel; this is the physical center of gravity of the body, and a center of psychic energy (Sanskrit, *câkra*). In martial arts, this is known as the "one point" (Japanese, *hara*; Chinese, *t'an t'ien*) that directs the flow of the vital energy (Japanese, *ki*; Chinese, *chi*). Inhale and exhale through the nose, breathing naturally from one point.

The flow of your breath should be entirely natural; zazen does not entail any sort of controlled breathing. You should not force the breath or try to slow your breathing. As you continue to sit, you will find the natural rhythm of the breath becomes more relaxed and slower of its own accord. This is a natural process and should not be forced.

Counting the breaths is a useful centering exercise when beginning zazen. There are several methods, the simplest being to count exhalations from one to ten, then beginning over again. Though this sounds quite simple, it is actually difficult for the undisciplined mind when first beginning zazen. Continued counting of breaths leads to a deepening of awareness and concentration.

In any case, thoughts, emotions or physical sensations that arise are simply to be noticed. If you lose the count, start over at one. Do not bother with any frustration, anger or recrimination. Simply breathe fully, relaxing totally into the present moment, as experienced through the breath.

Solo Zazen

While it is very beneficial to practice zazen in a zendô and in the presence of the *sangha* (the spiritual community), the true fruits of Zen are realized in your own practice, in the cycle of your daily life, in your time of sitting alone. It is highly recommended that you establish a practice of sitting regularly at home every day, even if only for short periods of time. It is better to sit daily for ten minutes than to sit for thirty or forty-five minutes once a week.

You should always dress comfortably, in loose clothing that does not bind or restrict your circulation or breathing.

Kôan Practice

In the Zen tradition there are devices that help in the deepening of practice, called *kôans*. Literally, a kôan means "public case," a situation presented in pithy sayings or anecdotes, usually involving exchanges of words and/or actions between a Zen master and a practitioner, or between seasoned masters. Any given kôan is meant to cut through the discursive (and delusive) mind, and bring the practitioner to an intellectual impasse that may lead to a direct experience of reality that is non-conceptual.

Kôans are not to be taken up by anyone at random, but are given to a practitioner by an authorized Zen teacher as an aid toward the deepening of practice. The possibility of continued guidance and follow-up is presupposed when a teacher gives a kôan to a particular student.

In the Sanbô Kyôdan tradition (see Part II, Chapter 12, *Sanbô Kyôdan Lineage*), kôans are employed both as a help in leading practitioners to the initial awakening experience, and more importantly, as a way of deepening the experience toward its continued embodiement in one's daily life.

The kôan most commonly given to those who express a certain kind of attitude in practice described earlier as "having one's hair on fire" is the kôan *MU*. (For particulars, see *The Three Pillars of Zen*.) Other kôans may also be given to help open the eye of the practitioner, such as "The sound of one hand," or "Who hears?"

Practitioners who are not given kôans as such, but who are encouraged to continue zazen by counting, or paying attention to the breath, or to "just sit" in full attention, however, should not think they are missing anything in not working with a kôan.

Kôans are like a box of tools that can be employed for certain situations. Certain kinds of fruit, like the coconut, for example, may have a hard outer shell, and it would be helpful to use a knife of a particular length and sharpness to open it. In peeling a tangerine, however, one can use one's bare hands and finger, for there is no need to use a knife. Using a knife when there is no need to do so may just damage the fruit, or cut the hand of the one using the knife.

So it is with kôans. Some practitioners may be aided by this practice, but others may actually be hindered by their use. A discerning teacher will be able to gauge the state of mind of each practitioner and will offer what is most fitting for each one's practice.

6 Walking & Zen in Action

Walking Zen

It has been repeatedly noted that the practice of Zen is centered in, but not limited to, zazen or formal sitting meditation. Zen involves the totality of one's life, lived in full awareness of the present moment in every situation.

The quality of one's practice then makes itself manifest in the way one's awareness becomes transformed in one's ordinary life, in one's activities, in one's attitudes, in one's ways of relating to the world. This is what we refer to by "Zen in action."

The connecting point between zazen and Zen in action can be found in the meditative walk between periods of zazen. In this form of Zen, one is encouraged to be fully aware of each movement of one's body, breathing deeply with each step, slowly and deliberately.

In a typical session, periods of zazen are interspersed with walking meditation, known as *kinhin* in Japanese. This provides welcome relief for joints and muscles. However, the brief time spent in kinhin is not meant to be a break in the process of meditation. Rather, it is an effective mode of meditation between the seated mode of zazen and the Zen awareness in the midst of one's daily activities.

As you walk slowly and deliberately, you should remain totally aware of the present: your breath, your balance, your walking step by step.

Posture

To practice walking Zen, stand erect but relaxed. Form a fist with one hand by tucking the thumb to the palm, then folding the fingers over the thumb. This hand is then placed at the solar plexus region (the slight cavity at the base of the ribs), with the fist vertical. The other hand is then placed over the fist, also remaining vertical.

The body can "sink" slightly by bending the knees; this helps localize attention in the body's natural center of gravity, known as the "one point," (Japanese, *hara*; Chinese, *t'an t'ien*). As you walk, be aware of the totality of walking, the shifting of balance, all the while moving consciously from the center of your being.

Walk slowly, lifting each foot and placing it on the floor very deliberately and precisely. Shift the weight forward until balance is achieved, then lift the other foot. If your center is good, you can balance on one foot, feeling the fluid motion of walking, the exquisite and subtle shift of balance. If your energy is focused in your head, you might tend to wobble or teeter as you move forward. You can focus your attention at the *hara*, the physical center of gravity, located approximately two inches below the navel.

Those who have had some experience in the martial arts (especially Tai Chi or Aikidô) or yoga will find some proficiency in the slow, deliberate and balanced walking meditation.

Non-action in Action

Walking is an activity we do so much in our daily life, whether it be simply walking from the living room to the dining room, or taking a walk in a park or a shopping mall. These times can be occasions for us to return to a centered mode of awareness similar to the walk between periods of zazen.

The formalized way of walking meditation enables us to be fully aware of our bodily movements and of our breathing during the process. This experience of being in a formal state of meditation while in action (walking) can gear us to a mode of awareness wherein we are fully centered in the here and now in the midst of our activities.

In other words, the practice of Zen is not limited to formal seated meditation (zazen), but encompasses all of one's activities and passivities in daily life. It involves a mode of awareness that is maintained throughout the day, in a way that is, paradoxically speaking, intentional but effortless. It is a mode of being that can be described as non-action in action. One can gradually "taste" this mode of being as one continues in regular zazen practice, letting its fruits outflow into one's daily life.

Zen and Socio-ecological Action

It has been repeatedly emphasized that Zen practice, though centered in, is not confined to zazen or seated meditation, but rather involves a mode of awareness that encompasses one's whole life. One's daily life is the field wherein the unitive (nondual) awareness of Zen comes to bear fruit.

This awareness is of an intrinsic interconnectedness with all sentient beings. It leads one to experience the pains and sorrows, as well as the joys and hopes, of one's fellow beings as one's very own. This awareness can thus empower a Zen person to action toward socio-ecological transformation. As one experiences the pain of victims of violence and injustice and ecological destruction as one's very own pain, active engagement toward their alleviation becomes the most natural way of life for such a person.

A Zen person's activity in this dimension can also be called the action of non-action, since, from the Zen standpoint, there is no one acting, there is no one on whose behalf one is acting, and there is no action whatsoever. Such action of non-action is likened to that of one "straightening one's pillow with the outstretched hand in the middle of the night" (Blue Cliff Records, No.89). In other words, without any trace of self-consciousness or self-righteousness, one simply does what needs to be done, as the most natural thing in the world to do at that very moment.

7 Zendô Etiquette

The Zendô

The *zendô* (literally, place of Zen) is simply the room or location set aside for zazen. The setting is spacious, and sparsely furnished, conducive to meditation and introspection. This setting is influenced by the Zen aesthetic and formal Japanese Zen monasteries and temples, so zendôs usually contain examples of Zen art or calligraphy, perhaps a small statue of Buddha.

Each Zen community would have it's own specific customs, or "zendô etiquette," but the following are considerations that would apply in general.

Gasshô and Bowing

As one enters the zendô, one stops before the altar to bow before taking one's place, with hands in the *gasshô* position. Gasshô is a traditional sign of respect, found in many Eastern customs, religions, and martial traditions.

Gasshô is a Japanese term which means "palms joined." The palms of both hands are placed together before the face, fingertips about the level of the nose.

When performing gasshô, you are showing respect to the teachers, the teaching, and the community (*sangha*). It is traditional to bow and perform gasshô towards your place of meditation before each period of zazen; this act honors your practice, an acknowledgment of respect for your intrinsic Buddha nature.

At the end of *sesshins* (encounter of the heart; extended periods of intense zazen lasting from three days to one week), a series of full body prostrations is sometimes practiced.

In the West, bowing is unknown and foreign. However, it is a much more intimate and honoring gesture than shaking hands. Bowing to others or even to an image of the Buddha is not idol worship or a debasing of oneself; it is an acknowledgment of the compassionate or wisdom aspect of the True Self. A Zen master (Kosho Uchiyama) has described the act of bowing to an image of the Buddha as the recognition within yourself of the embodiment of zazen, and by extension, of your True Self.

Bowing signifies acknowledgment and respect to the higher self within one and others, that power driving one towards awakening.

When in the zendô, an attitude of formality, respect and especially consideration of others is expected. If anyone is engaged in zazen, conversation or other distractions are inappropriate and should be conducted in the hallway or the rooms reserved for the introductory lectures.

Formal Zazen

During zazen, it is extremely important to remain still. This is important in developing your own practice, but in the community setting of the zendô, any movement or noise is distracting for others.

In the early stages of zazen, the restlessness of the mind is often reflected in the body as physical tension, tightness or pain. After some proficiency is gained in zazen, these sensations are no longer distractions; they can be noticed and observed without any "relief" action required by the body.

In the event you receive a "call of nature," you can exit the zendô during walking zen. When you return, enter the line at the place you were previously.

The desired atmosphere of stillness in the zendô during zazen is often interrupted by various sounds. These could include the activities of the monitor as postures are checked, the coming or going of students to *dokusan*, or the typical external sounds of any metropolitan area: jets, traffic, sirens, birds, rain etc. These sounds are simply to be observed; they are nothing more than the expression of the totality of the moment and of the content of your mind, no matter what form they take.

In any event, what is happening in the environment as you sit in zazen is the absolute expression of the moment. There is nothing special to deal with or change, nothing to be distracted by, nothing even to observe. The moment is; that's all.

Dokusan

Dokusan is a formal, one-to-one teacher-student interview. This is a very important aspect of practice. It enables the practitioner, as it were, to look at oneself in a mirror and see what is happening in one's practice through the eyes and with the help of an experienced teacher. Dokusan allows for the testing and tempering of one's experiences of insight or awakening.

After students complete the introductory talks, they are eligible for dokusan. Upon a request to the monitor, they are presented to the teacher for the first interview.

What goes on in dokusan is a confidential matter based on a covenantal relationship between teacher and student. The teacher is bound by confidentiality concerning formal dokusan contents regarding matters of Zen practice, seeking only the greatest well-being of the student in every case. The student is thereby also expected to respect this confidentiality and not divulge particulars to other persons, as it may hinder these in their own spiritual path.

Teishô

Teishô (literally, "recited offering") is the traditional Zen talk by the teacher, typically delivered at specified times. The topics usually relate to some aspect of practice.

Teishô is a verbal expression of the essence of Zen in the moment. These talks are delivered in the fullness of the present. A formal meditation posture is recommended for listening to the teishô, including a respectful and attentive state of mind. You should listen to the teishô as if this is a one-to-one communication, addressed specifically to you, and covering topics that are intimately related to your practice.

Chanting

Chanting is an important part of community zazen practice. The rhythm of the chants, the participation with others in harmony, the texts of the sûtras as vehicles of meditation, are all important to deepening practice.

In most zendos, the basic chants used include the *Kanzeon (Kannon) Sûtra*, the *Heart Sûtra*, the Bodhisattva Vows, the Vow of Purification, Hakuin's *Song of Zazen*, and the *Chant on the Identity of Relative and Absolute*. The texts of these chants are well worth reading and can be a great aid in your practice.

Tea

At the conclusion of zazen and chanting, tea is sometimes served. Designated servers bring the tea into the zendô, first presenting tea at the altar and then serving the teacher, if present. Tea is served in silence, offering each practitioner the opportunity to "savor the moment" in the company of the sangha.

In conclusion, the zendô is a place for formal zazen practice. The formality and silence observed can offer a conducive atmosphere for a genuine "encounter of the heart."

8 Sesshin

Encounter of the Heart

Sesshins are special periods of intense zazen, typically lasting from three to seven days, and sometimes longer. The word sesshin literally means "encounter of the heart." In other words, "touching the core of one's being." This is an actualization of one of the four marks of Zen (see Chapter 1, *What is Zen?*, page 4), "direct pointing to the human mind and heart," which can open one's eyes to see one's true nature as awakened.

The following guidelines are presented to help in maintaining mindfulness during sesshin:

- Keep silence at all times. Do not speak or make physical gestures to anyone. In deference to others, always try to avoid making any unnecessary sounds. You are expected to remain silent everywhere. If you have any questions or problems, please address them to the monitor. No one is allowed to use a phone unless it is an emergency or matter of serious importance.

- Keep your eyes lowered. Eye contact is distracting during sesshin; you will already be connected to others at a deeper level. Be self-contained. Carry your silence and attention to your movements in each moment of the sesshin.

- There will be *samu* (work chores), and you will be given specific tasks. Take these assignments as part of practice and be fully present in each task.

- Be on time for all scheduled activities. The clappers or bell will be used as signals for group activity. You are expected to be at the zendô at least five minutes before zazen. Avoid coming to the zendô late, as it is distracting to others. Inform the monitor if you are unable to sit at any given period of zazen.

- Zendô etiquette:
  - Always bow at the door as you enter or leave.
  - Never walk directly across the center of the zendô. To cross to the other side, walk down the aisle to the back of the zendô, then continue around to the other side. If you pass in front of the altar, pause briefly to gasshô toward the altar.
  - Each time you rise for kinhin, fluff your zafu (sitting cushion) and place it in the center of the zabuton (sitting mat), aligned with the other zafus. This will keep the zendô atmosphere orderly and visually correct, and provide you an additional opportunity to maintain mindfulness as you transition from zazen to kinhin.

- During the teishô, maintain an erect posture and straight back. Keep your hands in the formal zazen mudra, or relax them with the left hand over the right. If you need to change position, do so quietly and in a mindful manner, without attracting undue attention. Remember to listen to the teishô as if the talk were directed to you personally.
- During chanting, if you read from the prepared text, hold it properly between your thumbs and forefingers in the gasshô position. Place the text beneath your zabuton when chanting is finished.

• Kentan. In its literal sense, means "inspection of the mat." Each morning at the beginning of the first sitting, the teacher will enter the zendô and walk around to check individual postures and the "presence" of each sitter. Participants will already be seated in zazen, facing the wall. The teacher will first light incense and then make three prostrations. When the teacher is finished, the monitor will shout "Kentan!" The teacher will then approach the monitor and gasshô, after which the teacher will walk slowly behind each sitter. As the teacher approaches your back, place your hands in the gasshô position to signal readiness. Immediately after the teacher passes, return your hands to the formal zazen position.

• Kinhin. Participants will walk in a circle during kinhin. As you walk, pace yourself to the person in front of you; do not lag behind at your own pace. If you need to use the bathroom, you may do so during kinhin, after the gasshô. When you return, join the kinhin circle. Return before the formal sitting bell is rung.

- Dokusan. The teacher will ring the bell as the signal for you to enter the dokusan room. Walk briskly to the door and wait for the person inside to open the door. Remain outside; when the door is opened, wait for the person to turn to face the teacher, then gasshô together to the teacher. When the person leaves, enter the dokusan room. The person exiting will close the door. Go to your position on the zabuton in front of the teacher, and after you assume the zazen position, gasshô again to the teacher. When your interview is finished, the teacher will ring the bell. Gasshô to the teacher while still on the zabuton, then rise and walk slowly backward to the door. Open the door, gasshô again to the teacher with the person who is waiting outside. Perform all movements in the dokusan room slowly and with complete mindfulness. If there are any special instructions regarding dokusan, these will be announced prior to the first interview.

- Tea. Tea should be taken in complete silence. A server will approach two persons at the same time, and they will gasshô in unison. The server will offer the cup tray to the first person, who takes a cup. The server then offers a cup to the remaining person, then all three gasshô in unison. This routine is repeated around the zendô, until all participants have tea cups.

The tea server repeats this procedure. Hold the empty cup in the palm of your right hand as the tea is poured; when you have the desired amount, signal to the server by raising your left hand, palm up. Again, the tea server and the two participants will gasshô in unison. Place the cup of tea on the floor directly in front of you. Do not drink until everyone has been served. When the monitor sounds the clappers, the whole zendô will gasshô together. You may then drink your tea. When you have finished, place the empty cup on the floor. The tea ceremony is concluded by chanting "Shalom" three times. The cup server will return to collect the cups.

• Proper clothing. Wear loose, dark clothing at all times. Sleeveless shirts, leotards, and shorts are not allowed. Do not use any perfume, after-shave, cologne, or body oils that would be noticeable to others.

• Meals. All meals will be taken together in the dining hall. Everyone will walk in order, in a single line to the dining room. Keep your hands in the kinhin position. Remain standing until signaled to sit by the monitor. Shalom will be chanted at all meals, and this will be signaled by the monitor. Maintain mindfulness while eating. It is recommended that you eat only two-thirds of your normal intake of food. Eat with maximum efficiency and minimal motion; eat slowly. Maintain a straight back and correct posture. Avoid eye contact, and do not make any unnecessary gestures. If you reach the same place at the same time as another, allow the other to go first. At all times, remain inwardly concentrated.

- Posture correction. Occasionally, the monitor will walk around the zendô to correct postures and offer an encouraging "slap" or "thump" on the shoulders. If you want to get corrected, place your hands in the gasshô position to signal the monitor that you need encouragement. Do not bow. If you specifically do not want encouragement, touch your right shoulder with your left hand.

- Miscellaneous considerations.
  - Wait for the sound of the clappers before you rise in the morning. Do not use an alarm clock, as this will disturb roomates.
  - Turn all digital alarm watches off. Do not bring beepers, cellular phones, or other electronic devices to the sesshin, unless for medical reasons or prior agreement with the monitor and teacher.
  - Do not eat or drink in the sleeping quarters, or at any time other than the formal observed dining times. You can serve yourself hot or cold beverages from the dining hall during any free time. Do not bring alcoholic beverages to the sesshin under any circumstances.
  - As you walk around the grounds where the sesshin is being held, maintain the kinhin posture, especially as you go to dokusan.

- Place your shoes in a mindfull manner in the designated place before you enter the zendô. Keep all personal items away from the zabutons.
- Shower and bathe only during the scheduled times. Be brief with bathroom necessities, as there probably will be others waiting.
- At all times during the sesshin, but especially for any activities when in the zendô (teishô, tea, etc.), maintain an alert and erect posture.
- Except for those working on specific tasks assigned by the teacher, do not read or write during the sesshin.

A sesshin can provide a valuable opportunity for individuals to reach new levels of deepening and realization in the context of intensive practice. Serious students of Zen are encouraged to participate in sesshin at least once or twice a year, in addition to their regular zazen in daily life. New "breakthroughs" or "openings" are more likely to happen either during, or very soon after a sesshin.

Beginning Zen

9 The Role of the Zen Teacher

Teaching and Practice

In Zen practice, one cannot emphasize enough the vital role of the Zen teacher who has charted the paths of this arduous journey to the core of one's being and is familiar with the terrain. There is a proliferation of literature on the matter that may just leave the individual seeking a handle or practical guide as to what Zen is all about all the more confused. The opportunity to receive guidance from an authentic Zen teacher can make all the difference in getting through the maze.

A teacher assists in the process whereby participants are enabled to let go of their baggage and come to a fundamental experience of "seeing into one's true nature," a liberating experience that transforms the individual practitioner's whole way of seeing, of relating, of being.

Thus one may liken the teacher's role to that of a midwife who has been of assistance in the birthing of a new life. The midwife is by no means the source of that life, but is simply one who sees to it that the way is cleared and the conditions made favorable for the new life to come through and see the light. Each birth is indeed a joyous and exciting event, filled with a fresh sense of wonder and mystery.

The teacher-disciple relationship in Zen involves a covenant whereby the teacher agrees to render to the disciple whatever is called for or necessary in enabling the disciple to live more fully the life of oneness and interconnectedness that Zen practice opens one to. In turn, the disciple takes the teacher as a person to look to for guidance in such a vital matter as one's journey in encountering the mystery of one's very being.

In presenting oneself to a particular teacher in Zen, it is understood that the disciple will take this teacher's word to be authoritative in matters relating to Zen practice and will not turn to other teachers to seek help on the same matters while one remains in this covenant.

This is especially important for those who are beginning in this practice and need a decisive guiding hand to lead them in this rigorous practice involving a perilous process. Going from one teacher or director to another may only confuse the practitioner, as different teachers inevitably have different styles in their direction of others, and there may be conflicting points in the details of practice given to the same individual.

To avoid such confusion on the part of the beginning practitioner, it is of prime importance that the disciple follow the guidance of one teacher that she or he feels confident in being able to show the way, rather than looking for a second opinion on spiritual matters.

However, if the practitioner somehow begins to feel that this particular teacher may not be the one best suited for oneself, then the practitioner is always free to express this, bid farewell to the teacher, and go to another with whom the practitioner can resonate better. Such a case then is not a breaking, but a concluding of the covenant, and the practitioner is then free to begin another one. In doing so, she/he is enjoined to set aside and forget everything received from the former teacher, lest anything stand in the way of full acceptance of the guiding hand of the newly chosen teacher, who inevitably would have a different style of direction.

A true teacher does not make an issue of a disciple's departure and, in fact, wishing only the practitioner's greatest good, is ready to help the latter in finding another teacher who may be of better help. The guiding principle for the teacher in such cases is to translate a famous Japanese proverb: *Kuru mono wo kobamazu, saru mono wo owazu* ("not refusing those who come, not pursuing those who go").

Zen spirituality can be described simply as "the art of living in attunement with the Breath," and it is the Breath itself that will be the most reliable guide in the entire journey. Ultimately, the task of the Zen teacher is to help the practitioner be tamed by the Breath, to be fully given over to its healing and transforming power.

- excerpted from *Healing Breath*
(Orbis Books), pp. 48-50

Beginning Zen

10 The Stages of the Path

The Child in Us - Zen Oxherding Pictures

The Zen oxherding pictures help us mirror where we are in our practice. One preliminary point in looking at these ten oxherding pictures is to realize that they are "stages" not in the linear sense that the latter stages are superior to the earlier stages. We see them precisely as an invitation to jump into the circle of enlightenment.

They are indications that enable us to see where we are in the circle. But this should not lead us to think, "Ah, I'm better than that one because I am in number six and that other person is just in number three!" So we are not to see it in a way that merely puffs up our ego.

On the other hand, we need not demean ourself and say, "Oh, I'm only in number two, and so-and-so is already in number six or number seven." We are invited to see it as traversing a circular path, where we are in a community together with all sentient beings, and we are finding our place in this community in a unique and irreplaceable way.

The circle, as we know from our understanding of Zen tradition, is a representation of our true self. And it is written in Chinese or Japanese calligraphy in a way that is not exactly mathematically perfect, that is, in a way that every point is equidistant from the center. Instead, it is written given all the contours of the human hand who wrote it. <u>That itself</u>, with all the contours, is supposed to be the manifestation of perfection, not the mathematically correct figure where every point in the circle is equidistant from the center.

The circle is drawn by a human hand, with a brush, and is perfect just as it is. And one other feature of this circle that you will note if you really look at genuine Zen work closely is that it is not a closed circle. There is always a slight opening somewhere and that indicates that it is not something that is contained in itself, but opens out to space, to infinity.

With that in the background, we can look at the circle, as an invitation for us to ask, "Who am I?" and "How can I discover that the true self as represented by a circle in me in a way that I can see myself also as open in that dimension of infinite?" And if you take the cue from the circle it also represents... nothing. Precisely because there is nothing in it, it is also perfect and complete, just as it is. So these two elements — fully empty and yet totally replete — just as it is — are the picture of our true self.

The first picture depicts a little child who is supposed to be perplexed, or is searching for something. "In the beginning, suddenly emerged from confusion." Another description of this same first picture of a child just beginning to open its eyes and wonder about things is "the awakening of the fact." So it is the first stage in the awakening process asking the question: "What's this all about?"

This is already a very significant step. Before the first stage there is already a kind of awakening, namely, a mind that begins asking questions. One becomes aware that one is perplexed in asking "Who am I?" "How can I live my life in a way that is meaningful?" or "What is the meaning of all this?"

Before arriving at this stage, perhaps we have been asleep many years, taking things in life for granted. We were once a child, then a teenager, and then we move on to adulthood, just following the normal stages and routines of human living. We may have gotten married and have started a family, and so on, and then suddenly, at some point in our lives, we begin to ask the big questions. It may come when we are thirty or forty or even fifty. Or, it may come for some of us at an earlier age.

The child in the picture represents that stage that now begins to awaken and ask, "What is this all about?" So the asking of the question leads us to seek some form of practice that will enable us to pursue those questions.

Struggling to emerge from confusion

The second stage is described as "finding the ox's traces." Now one gets a sense of where one may go in pursuing that question and is inspired to go on further. The ox here is also a symbol of the true self in the same way that the circle also is the true self. And so now one sees traces, like hoof prints: "Oh, there must be something that makes this life worth living, so let me see what it is."

One begins asking more questions and may begin reading some books, going to talks on spirituality, and so on. Or one may go to a religious center, or join a group to pursue some kind of practice that will deepen our sense of awareness and goad us on in our search.

2
Sighting the tracks

The third stage is the sighting of the ox. Perhaps we may not yet see the whole ox, but we may glimpse its tail, or some part of the ox, that makes us sure that the ox is certainly there. But yet we haven't seen it fully yet. The glimpse just whets our appetite, and leads us to go further.

In the Zen tradition, this third stage is known as the initial opening, or *kenshô* experience. This is the initial experience of awakening to the true self. We may have only a brief glimpse — but at least we know that it is there. Now we know, not just from hearsay or from others who have seen it, or not just from deducing it from the tracks we may have seen or the ox manure we may have smelled along the way. But having directly seen it, we know that it is there and so we are given a new impetus to follow it. And so for those of us who may have had a new experience like this, so suddenly, coming to us like this, we may say, "Now I've got it! Now, I have this kenshô and so I'm fully in the Zen light!"

Well, hear this: that is just the beginning of it. The sighting of it may still relapse into a memory and therefore, it can become just an ego trip, and you may claim yourself as an enlightened person. But that will just put another block in the journey itself. So, that's why in our center we do not make such a big fuss about that initial experience. It is like an initial sighting that should simply draw us on to look further.

3

Glimpsing the Wild Cow

The fourth stage is now the catching of the ox. After having sighted it we go closer to it and are maybe even able to lasso it and, as the picture in one version shows, the little child holds a rope around the ox's neck. Now, we have the ox closer at hand.

But still the ox is unwieldy and it can still run away from us. It is still not under control. We have a rope that can enable us to keep it in tow. But still we have to continue to exert effort to enable it to stay there and not to run away from us.

4

Catching the Cow to turn it around

In the fifth stage then, is one in which the ox has been tamed somewhat, and we are able to live in peace with it. It even follows us, and now we are leading the ox along the path.

We are now a little more accustomed to practice, and are now beginning to experience a sense of peace, a sense of joy. An inner satisfaction begins to make itself felt in our daily life, manifesting itself in our way of being more compassionate and being more thoughtful of others, and so on. And we begin to receive the fruits of the practice with less and less effort on our part.

5

Leading the cow on the path

The sixth stage is riding the ox home. We are now able to feel that we are on our way home. We can ride the ox and it doesn't try to jump and throw us away like a bucking bronco anymore. It is now fully one with us and we are comfortable riding the ox. But still, there is more to come.

6

Riding the Cow home

The seventh stage talks about the ox forgotten: leaving the child to simply sit there and meditate deeply. So now, even the ox is gone. At this stage one is no longer thinking about oneself, no longer having to pursue words like "dharma" or "enlightenment" and so on. We are home and we don't need to think about looking for something else. We are comfortable where we are.

7

Cow forgotton, leaving the girl to meditate

At the eighth stage, both the boy and the ox are forgotten. There is an empty circle represented here. There is no longer any ox, that is, no longer any sense of conceptualizing "truth" or "dharma" or "true self" or whatever. There is also no subject (I, me, mine) attempting to conceptualize or verbalize those terms. Both the subject and object are gone.

In the eighth stage, the concepts of truth, God, holiness, dharma, and so on have disappeared, and you're simply living life in its pure simplicity. The eighth is a stage where even thoughts about yourself are no longer there. In some versions of the oxherding pictures, this eighth stage is presented as the last stage.

Both girl and cow forgotten!

The ninth stage is described as a return to nature. Now, after having forgotten both the object and the subject, what appears? There's a bamboo shoot, there is a plum blossom, a rock beside a gently flowing stream. Further than that we don't see. Just the realization of the way things are, as they are, in their naturalness. It is simply realizing that plum blossoms are there, and they are just what they are. All the things in life are seen with eyes of wonder, taken just for what they are.

9

Return to the source

But the tenth stage is the fullness and completion of the full ten stages. And what does this depict? Here we see the child again, in playful mirth. In India the statues of the Buddha are usually emaciated, giving a sense of asceticism and world-renunciation, of transcendence. In China however, the pictures of the Buddha are always associated with mirth and laughter and gaiety. So he is depicted as a very rolly-polly person, always laughing and always happy.

10

Meeting Laughing Buddha on Life's Playful Road

And so the Chinese deity of happiness and mirth came to be identified with the figure of the Buddha. So this tenth stage is experiencing that sense of joy and mirth and playfulness in one's daily life, no matter what. Another depiction of this stage is the return to the market place. We are back in the concrete struggles of our daily life. And yet, we are now able to live them, live right in the midst of them, with a sense of playfulness. We transcend our struggles not be escaping them, but by plunging ourselves right into them with a new sense of freedom and a sense of humor and a sense of acceptance.

This is a summary of the ten oxherding pictures to help us realize that there are different stages along the way. We can truly say "It is good to be, every step along the way." We keep coming back full circle: it is always the child in us that draws us to all this.

So what we are invited to do is — keep returning to that child in us, the one who can partake of the gifts of being. And as we can see from the title of the book written by the Japanese Zen teacher Shunryu Suzuki, *Zen Mind Beginner's Mind*, that is the place that we are always invited to return, that is, come back full circle to where we have been all along.

There is no sense putting on airs, thinking "Now I've advanced along the path." Yet again, we need not downplay our practice thinking, "I still have a long ways to go." We can realize both aspects, but yet we also realize that it is a circle that we are invited to simply plunge ourselves into and open our eyes to. As we do so, we know that at every step along the path, there is a fullness that we can experience. And yet, it is a fullness that doesn't let us stop there, but motivates us to take the next step, from fullness to fullness — through a continual process of emptying.

Every step is a step that brings us home, wherever we are. In other words, the spiritual path that Zen invites us to take is no other than our own journey home. T.S. Elliot's poem is a succinct expression of this path:

> *We shall not cease from exploration*
> *And the end of all our exploring*
> *Will be to arrive where we started*
> *And know the place for the first time.*

Part II

The Lineage

11 A Brief History of Zen

The Historical Buddha

The practice of Zen grew out of the ground of the experience of Gautama of the Sâkya clan of India (563-483 BCE). As the son of local ruler, Gautama led a privileged and sheltered life, kept in ignorance of poverty, death, disease and aging by his father. One day, he left the palace without the permission or awareness of his father and saw a beggar, an old person, a sick person, and a dead person.

This experience was such a shock that Gautama renounced his inheritance and resolved to understand the meaning of life and death. He spent many years studying various forms of yoga and meditation with many masters and practicing asceticism, with no results. Disenchanted, he finally broke with all systems of teaching and all masters and retired to meditate beneath a bodhi-tree, resolving not to move until he came to realization. Legend records that after deep reflection, upon glimpsing the morning star, Gautama awakened to his true nature. After this experience, Gautama became known as the "Buddha."

The term Buddha means "the awakened one." Though recognizing that his experience of awakening was ineffable and unteachable, the Buddha realized that teaching could nevertheless be offered to those who sought it. Gautama began instruction in his experience; this became known as "turning the wheel of the Dharma." He formulated the principles of his realization in The Four Noble Truths and the path to realization and liberation in the "Middle Way" (that is, the balanced way of practice, between the extremes of total immersion in the world of the senses or the way of asceticism, total removal from the world).

The legendary transmission of Zen began with one of the Buddha's lectures to his disciples. In this particular instance, as the gathering waited for the traditional discourse, the Buddha remained silent; instead of speaking, he simply held a single flower aloft. The assembly of monks were puzzled and awaited the traditional lecture or explanation; the Buddha continued to keep silence.

Only the disciple Kâshyapa smiled in realization of the nature of this teaching. The Buddha smiled along with Kâshyapa, acknowledging Kâshyapa's realization and passing on the silent transmission of the Dharma Eye. Kâshyapa, also known as Mahakâshyapa, is recognized as the first patriarch of Zen.

Bodhidharma

Zen traces its direct lineage to the legendary figure of Bodhidharma (Chinese, Ta' Mo; Japanese, Daruma). Legend and history are inseparably intertwined in the imposing and mythical figure of Bodhidharma. He is recognized as the twenty-eighth Indian Zen patriarch, and the first Ch'an (Zen) patriarch in China.

This imposing figure arrived in China from India in the 6th century AD. After a long and difficult journey, Bodhidharma encountered Emperor Wu, the founder of the Liang dynasty, a supporter of Buddhism and a builder of many temples. Emperor Wu wanted acknowledgment of his virtue in the construction of Buddhist temples and his observance of the *Sûtras* (Sanskrit; literally, "strands"; teachings).

When Wu asked of Bodhidharma the merit of his deeds, Bodhidharma informed the emperor that these actions warranted no merit whatsoever. Wu then demanded what constituted true merit. Bodhidharma informed the emperor that true merit consisted of pure wisdom, wonderful and perfect; its essence emptiness, beyond the merit of worldly means. When the emperor asked what was sacred truth, Bodhidharma is reported to have replied, "Vast emptiness, nothing sacred." Wu then demanded to know who it was that spoke to him, whereupon Bodhidharma replied "Don't know" and ended the audience. Wu later realized the value of Bodhidharma's teachings and sent his daughter to study with him; she became one of his four main disciples.

Bodhidharma eventually settled in the country, engaged in hours of zazen. Legend maintains that he sat facing a wall for nine years, "listening to the ants scream." Students began to gather and then became disciples; the temple that grew from this community was the Shaolin Temple, which is also recognized as the legendary birthplace of certain forms of martial arts. Bodhidharma thus is recognized as the First Patriarch of Zen in China and the father of Shaolin style martial arts. Bodhidharma formally recognized one of his disciples (Hui-k'o) with the transmission of the *Dharma* (Sanskrit; "Universal Way or Truth"). The historical transmission of Zen through this recognition of enlightenment is known as Dharma Transmission; all lineages of Zen trace their origin to Bodhidharma.

Rinzai and Sôtô Zen

Transmission of the Zen patriarchy originating with Bodhidharma continued in China. Zen eventually developed several variations, but two major traditions in China stand out and continued in Japan: the Lin-chi school (better known by the Japanese term Rinzai) and the Ts'ao-tung school (Japanese Sôtô). Both traditions adhere to the essence of Zen via the recognition of the awakening or enlightenment experience and Dharma transmission, but differ markedly in their approach.

Rinzai Zen is traditionally ascribed to the figure of Lin Chi (d.866). Lin Chi was known for his dynamic, eccentric and dramatic behavior. He is credited with a revitalization of Zen and the systemization of *kôan* practice (kôans are non-conceptual, non-logical mind puzzles or conundrums specifically designed to foster awakening). Rinzai Zen is known as the "sudden school," with a strong emphasis on the sudden experience of awakening or enlightenment through continuous kôan practice.

In Rinzai, adherents practice zazen facing the center of the zendô. Enni Ben'en and Hakuin Ekaku (1201-1280 CE) have been recognized as pivotal figures of Rinzai practice in Japan.

The name "Sôtô" is the Japanese equivalent of the Chinese House of Ts'ao Tung. This Chinese term is derived from the abbreviated combinations of the graphs of the Chinese Zen masters Tung-shan Liang chieh (807-869 CE) and Ts'ao-shan Pen-chi (840-901 CE). Dôgen Zenji (1200-1253 CE) is credited with transplanting Sôtô thought from China to Japan in the 13th Century.

Sôtô Zen emphasizes the gradual realization of the inherent Buddha nature through zazen, known as *shikan-taza* (just sitting) in its purest form. In traditional Sôtô practice, zazen is performed facing the wall of the zendô.

Beginning Zen

12 The Sanbô Kyôdan Lineage

Hakuun Yasutani and the Sanbô Kyôdan

In the early 1950's, Hakuun Yasutani Rôshi, the designated Dharma successor of Harada (Sôgaku) Rôshi, established the Sanbô Kyôdan (Order of Three Treasures). Having received Dharma transmission in both the Rinzai and Sôtô traditions, Yasutani Rôshi sought to revive the teaching and practice of Zen.

The Sanbô Kyôdan brought together elements of both Rinzai and Sôtô traditions. A strong emphasis was placed on the practice of zazen, both alone and in formal groups, in the Sôtô tradition of facing the wall, while the Rinzai observance of kôan practice and dokusan (private interviews with the teacher) was also included. Yasutani Rôshi opened the practice of Zen to non-monastic Buddhists and later to non-Buddhists, thereby developing lay training and opening the door to Zen practice for Westerners. As a result of Yasutani Rôshi's foresight, a revitalization of Zen was brought about, combining key elements of the Sôtô and Rinzai traditions.

Many lay Buddhists, Jews, Christians and agnostics were attracted to the practice of individual responsibility and training found in Zen. Yasutani Rôshi was very instrumental in the introduction of Zen practice to the

United States in the 1960s and 1970s. Insightful accounts of Yasutani Rôshi are found in *Nine Headed Dragon River* by Peter Matthiesen, *The Three Pillars of Zen* by Philip Kapleau and *How the Swans Came to the Lake: a History of Buddhism in America* by Rick Fields. Some of Yasutani Rôshi's comments on death, dying, rebirth and karma are included in Philip Kapleau's compilation *The Wheel of Death*.

Kôun Yamada

Yamada Rôshi was the designated successor of Yasutani Rôshi in the continuing lineage of the Sanbô Kyôdan. Yamada Rôshi was a businessman and lay practitioner of Zen who attained a very deep *kenshô* (experience of awakening). This experience is recounted in *The Three Pillars of Zen*, under the heading "Mr. K. Y., a Japanese executive, age 47." Kôun Yamada published a commentary on one of the most famous texts of Zen kôans, the *Mumonkon*, also known as *The Gateless Gate*. It was with Yamada Rôshi that Ruben Habito first began the practice of Zen, at the encouragement of his spiritual director in the Society of Jesus.

Fr. Hugo Enomiya-LaSalle

Fr. Enomiya-LaSalle was instrumental in opening doors of dialogue between the Christian and Buddhist faiths and of the exploration of Zen meditation within a contemplative Christian frame of reference. He began the practice of Zen in Japan in 1943 under the direction of

Harada Rôshi. Fr. Enomiya-LaSalle was authorized to teach Zen by Yamada Rôshi; he began teaching Zen meditation to Christians and conducting *sesshins* ("encounter with the heart," intensive zazen retreats). His book *The Practice of Zen Meditation* chronicles a series of spiritual talks given during a typical sesshin, accompanied by photographs. This excellent resource book also includes comparisons of terminology, meditation, and mystical experience in both the Christian and Zen traditions .

Ruben Habito

Ruben Habito began his practice of Zen in 1971 at the San'un Zendô in Kamakura, Japan, under the direction of Yamada Rôshi. Ruben began kôan practice and attended sesshins; in 1971, he experienced kenshô. Kenshô was confirmed by Kôun Yamada Rôshi and later by Yasutani Rôshi. Ruben was authorized to teach Zen in 1988. He formed the Maria Kannon Zen Center in Dallas, Texas shortly thereafter, beginning with a small group in his house. This group later formally incorporated as Maria Kannon Zen Center, a non-profit organization.

The Sanbô Kyôdan tradition continues to spread around the world. Numerous zendôs exist in Japan, the United States, the Philippines, Germany, India, Spain, Switzerland and Australia. A partial list of Sanbô Kyôdan teachers is included in the Appendix, *Mindful Resources.*

13 Maria Kannon Zen

Maria Kannon Zen Center

The name of Maria Kannon Zen Center is taken from the two leading figures of compassion from the Christian and Buddhist traditions; Mary or Maria from Christianity, and Kannon (Sanskrit Avalokitésvara; Chinese, Kuan Yin) from the Buddhist tradition. The representation of Maria Kannon derives from a unique historical time of persecution of Christians in Japan. The following paragraphs provide some background to the name of our zendô.

Maria Kannon

"Maria Kannon" was the name of a certain kind of religious figurine venerated in many areas of Japan during the period of persecution of Christians. At the time, civil authorities had banned the practice of Christianity throughout the country, and forcibly closed Japan to the outside world, except through a small port in Kyûshû that remained accessible to Dutch traders.

During this period of nearly three hundred years, every citizen was required to profess adherence to, and register membership with, a local Buddhist temple, or else face grave consequences. Many Christians who refused to comply with these demands were tortured and executed.

Some groups of Christians chose a way of external compliance; registering with a Buddhist temple and even installing Buddhist statues in their homes, but meeting regularly in secret to encourage one another and pray together, to keep their Christian faith alive. These "hidden Christians" continued to practice their faith from generation to generation through the years of prohibition. Their existence came to light after the reopening of Japan to the West in the nineteenth century.

In many of the houses where hidden Christians lived were found an image of Avalokitésvara, or Kannon in Japanese, the Buddhist embodiment of compassion. Yet on closer look, one could also see the figure of Mary the Blessed Mother in the same figure. The Bodhisattva of Compassion was a familiar figure in Buddhist temples and homes. Christians gathering in secret, however, were in the company of the Mother of their Saviour, to whom they would turn for intercession in prayer.

Recently, Christians in Japan, in the attempt to give expression to key Christian themes from within their culture, have looked to Maria Kannon for significance over and above the historical context. Maria Kannon is being accorded renewed expression of a mutually resonating theme in the Buddhist and Christian traditions: the theme of compassion in its cosmic dimensions.

It is in the context of such a renewed appreciation and new significance, and in he hope of birthing a new possibility, that we look to the image of Maria Kannon as inspiration for Zen practice that cuts across traditional lines of demarcation between the Buddhist and Christian traditions.

The Character of Maria Kannon Zen

Maria Kannon Zen derives from an authentic Zen lineage and is firmly based upon the four cardinal principles of Zen, leading to the maturation of the three fruits of Zen practice, that is, the deepening of concentration, seeing into one's true nature as the way to enlightenment, and the embodiment of the peerless way in one's daily life. This is brought about through the threefold structure of practice consisting of adopting a conducive posture, following one's breath, and focusing the mind to stillness in the here and now. As such it is no different from other forms of genuine Zen. The transformation of the practitioner into a totally liberated being that lives in the realization of interconnectedness in daily life is its ultimate fruit.

As such, it is found within the context of traditional Zen, but its particular accent I would say lies in two points: (a) its attempt to be open not only to Buddhist but also to Christian expressions in order to "point to the moon," as it were, that is, to lead practitioners to a veritable transformative experience, and (b) its emphasis on the activation of compassion as an essential component of Zen practice, as the natural outflow of that experience of seeing into one's own true nature.

Concerning (a), Yamada Rôshi himself has made use of Christian imagery and conceptual descriptions in many of his teishô or Zen talks, with the many Christian disciples in the audience in mind, to point to the implications and nuances of the Zen experience. Now that many of those Christian disciples are themselves given the authorization to teach and guide others in Zen, they are able to draw from their own inner experience and familiarity with Christian scriptures to guide their own Christian disciples toward the realization of or a deepening of the Zen experience. Some have begun to employ kôans taken from Christian sources. This is still at an experimental stage, but the rich imagery found in Christian scriptures and tradition serves as a fertile field for creativity in this regard, founded, of course, on the cardinal principle that Zen does not rely on words or letters, as it points directly to the core or center of our human being, where we come to touch the ultimate dimension.

Concerning (b), first of all, the understanding of compassion as the natural outflow of wisdom has been there since the beginnings of Mahayana Buddhism. Secondly, the Christian Gospel has been understood from the start as a message of divine compassion, and as an invitation to live one's life vivified by this compassion and to become an agent of its realization in history. Our age in particular, characterized by a global situation nearing a critical point, calls for a renewed emphasis on this fundamental religious impulse.

Maria Kannon Zen

This emphasis on the activation of compassion as a vital component and test for the genuineness of religious life is all the more imperative, in that many institutionalized forms of Zen, not to mention other forms of meditation, have given the impression of stopping at the "inward movement," that is, of being caught up in the rigorous disciplinary side of practice and glorifying in this aspect, to the point of not being able to carry out the implications of such practice in a life that realizes interconnectedness in concrète ways in the individual's daily life. In other words, the outflow into compassion as a significant fruit of practice needs to be manifested more clearly in the worldview and living relationships of Zen practitioners in a much clearer way.

As embodiments of this outflow of practice into living compassion, we have, of course, examples of notable figures such as Robert Aitken Rôshi, himself a direct disciple of Yamada Kôun Rôshi and founder of the Diamond Sangha Zen community based in Hawaii, as well as Thich Nhat Hanh and a few others. They succeed in drawing our attention to this crucial dimension of Zen and meditative practice in general, especially as this compassion leads to a peace-filled and ecologically sound way of life for all of us fellow members of our Earth community.

This is the dimension of practice that Maria Kannon Zen also hopes to place an accent on, and draw out in a more explicit way in the small but growing number of its regular practitioners.

95

This facet of practice is given expression in one of the kôans given in the Sanbô Kyôdan program of training to those who come to an initial experiential breakthough.

> Why is it that in the accomplished saints and bodhisattvas, crimson lines (of tears) never cease to flow?

This kôan is not meant to be solved by an intellectual explanation, but in an experiential grasp of that mystery that being born as a sentient being in this interconnected universe is all about. It is an expression of the mystery of the tears of Kannon. We can say also that it is an expression of the tears of Mary at the foot of the cross, in deepest sorrow and pain as she stands by her own Son, who bears the wounds of the universe in his own body.

- Ruben Habito
(*Buddhist Christian Studies,*
Vol . 14, 1994, pp. 145-150)

14 Is Zen a Religion?

Let me state my conclusion regarding the above question at the outset. I believe that Zen is not a religion in the ordinary sense. There are several reasons I can give for this.

First of all, that which is usually referred to as religion begins and ends with the element of faith. That is, religion conventionally starts with belief in an absolute or supreme being—God or Buddha, for example—who can either be the creator of the universe or dwell in our hearts. This faith is then deepened over the days and years until it becomes unshakable. I understand this as an absolute condition for religion in the traditional sense. As for Zen, although belief in an intrinsic and essential nature, infinite and absolute, is the start of practice, it is through realizing that infinite and absolute essential nature in the experience of satori that the need for belief vanishes. Or put more succinctly, Zen practice begins with belief and ends in actual experience. Here is an aspect of Zen that distinguishes it fundamentally from religions containing only the element of faith.

A second reason why Zen is not a religion is the absence of particular scriptures to depend on. Christianity has its Bible, Islam its Koran; even in Buddhism, the Hokke Sect has the Lotus Sûtra, the Kegon Sect the Kegon Sûtra and the Jôdo Sect the Jôdo Sûtra. These scriptures are all maintained and carefully preserved, and the interpretation of individual words and phrases has an extremely important meaning and significance. Although it would be inaccurate to say that writings in the Zen sect are not traditional scriptures, Zen is distinguished by lacking a single scripture upon which everything depends. And although we could stretch a point, perhaps, and say the *Hannyashingyô* ("Heart Sûtra") is such a traditional scripture, as long as study of this sûtra ends in intellectual discussion, it has no relation to Zen whatsoever.

Yet another reason why Zen is not a religion in the conventional sense is its very practical approach of negating all concepts. Although most religions also have a practical side known as prayer, this is usually a subjective action of the individual and not an organized system of practice. Instead, the most important role is played by the sermons of religious leaders, based mainly on inherited scriptures, or expositions of the meaning of individual words or phrases in those scriptures. Zen, however, negates all concepts; instead, the central focus is experience in which the fact is experienced as fact. Zen also has zazen, a concrete and practical method of adjusting the body, breath and spirit to realize truth. Zen has moreover developed methods of guidance toward realization in which we practice zazen to realize the fact as fact. In this respect Zen differs fundamentally from religions in the usual sense.

However, when we consider the matter carefully, is it enough in relieving human suffering and gaining true peace of mind to simply believe sacred scriptures that are a natural outpouring of the enlightenment experiences of the ancient worthies? Is it enough to be able to interpret individual phrases of those scriptures with unsurpassed skill or simply pray in that direction? When all is said and done, we cannot forego the five aspects of belief (*shin*), understanding (*ge*), practice (*gyô*), enlightenment (*shô*) and personalization (*nyû*). If peace of mind is truly a matter of believing and understanding a reality that we have made our own, we must practice ourselves and realize so that it becomes an immutable fact. We must then personalize that experience before we can live relatively free of worry. Viewed in this way, perhaps only Zen, with its aspects of practice and realization, can be called a religion in the true sense of the word.

In Case Nine of the Blue Cliff Record, a monk asks Jôshû, "What is Jôshû?"

Jôshû is also the name of the area where Jôshû Oshô lived. With his question, the monk is pressing Jôshû to reveal his enlightened state of consciousness.

In reply, Jôshû says, "East Gate, West Gate, South Gate, North Gate."

Because of the geographical place Jôshû has an east, west, south and north gate, Master Jôshû presents the monk directly with the geographical Jôshû . In Jôshû's consciousness, however, there are no gates at all. By his reply, Jôshû reveals his totally free state of consciousness, telling the monk to enter from any gate that he wishes and Jôshû will be a match for him. No matter what should enter by any one of the gates, the totally unfettered Jôshû is ready with an appropriate response at that time and place.

That is the reason why Zen can accept people of any religion, and why all people, regardless of their background, can deepen their state of consciousness through Zen practice and thus savor the true meaning of the religion they profess.

- by Kubota Jiun

(from *Kyôshô* No. 23,
Sept.-Oct. 1991
translated by Paul Shepherd)

15 Zen Practice and Christians

I am often asked by Christians, especially Catholics, whether they can practice zazen, and still preserve the beliefs of Christianity. To that question, I usually answer that Zen is not a religion, in the same sense that Christianity is a religion. Therefore, there is no reason why Christianity and zazen cannot coexist.

Almost all Buddhist sects can be called religions. Zazen however, is quite different in this respect. Quite simply, it is the core of all Buddhist sects. As you know, there are many sects in Buddhism, but the core or essence of them all is the experience called satori or self-realization. The theories and philosophies of all the sects are but the clothing covering the core. These outer wrappings are of various shapes and colors, but what is inside remains the same. And the core, this experience, is not adorned with any thought or philosophy. It is merely a fact, an experienced fact, in the same way that the taste of tea is a fact. A cup of tea has no thought, no idea, no philosophy. It tastes the same to Buddhists as it does to Christians. There is no difference at all.

You may ask what makes this experience happen. Well, quite simply, it is when certain conditions are present to the consciousness of a human being, and a reaction occurs. This reaction we call the Zen experience. This reaction we call the Zen experience. The reaction of this experience is always the same, regardless of the beliefs we may hold or the color of our skin. It could be compared to playing billiards. When we hit the balls with the same amount of power and in the same direction, all the balls roll along the same course and at the same angles, regardless of their color.

Now you may ask, what are the conditions that bring our consciousness to the experience. It is to concentrate with our mind in one-pointedness, and to forget ourselves in it. The one-pointedness is achieved sometimes in breath-counting, sometimes in what we call "following the breath," sometimes just sitting, and sometimes working on kôans. You will notice that all these ways point inwardly. It is a very interesting fact, but when we concentrate on an object outside ourselves, for example as in archery where we aim at a target, no matter how strong the concentration may be, we cannot attain the Zen experience. So in Zen practice, when we want to attain satori, we have to be absorbed inwardly.

Here you must remember, that the experience attained by zazen practice is not a thought or a philosophy or a religion, but merely a fact, a happening. And strange as it may seem, the experience of that fact has the power to free us from the agonies of the pains of the world. It emancipates us from the anxiety of all worldly sufferings. No one knows why that experience has such wonderful power, but it does. This is the most important point, and it's the most difficult to try to explain.

In the Zen experience, a certain unity happens, subject and object become one, and we come to realize our own self-nature. This self-nature cannot be seen, it cannot be touched, it cannot be heard. Because of these characteristics, we refer to is an "empty" (in Japanese, *ku*) but its activities are infinite. So, we say the Zen experience is the realization of the empty-infinite of our self-nature of our essential-nature, as it is often called.

When this happens, the fact is accompanied by a great peace of mind. At that moment, we feel as though the heavy burdens we have been carrying in our heart or on our shoulders, indeed all over our body and soul, suddenly disappear as if thrown away. The joy and happiness at that time is beyond all words. And there are no philosophies or theologies attached to it.

Should such a fact be called a religion? I don't think so. It is called satori, or self-realization, or enlightenment. Catholics are attaining the satori experience here in this zendô. I feel that in the future they should do research into the meaning or the origin of the fact of satori from the Christian's point of view. (This should be the work of Catholics and not mine.)

Having discovered this new world, the Zen student must learn that it is essentially one with the phenomenal world we all know so well. In my teaching I often use a fraction as an illustration to show that all things have two aspects, but are essentially one. In the fraction, the numerator is anything in the phenomenal world, a dog or cat, a finger or a flower, or Mary or Jiro. The denominator is the world of the empty-infinite which we call the essential world. Since the horizontal 8 expresses infinity in mathematics, I use it encircled by a zero as the denominator. The fraction is a way of expressing two aspects as one.

Regarding the relation between Christianity and Zen, I think it can be thought of as two highways, going in separate paths, but crossing at an interchange. The two roads may seem quite apart, but where they cross is common ground. Now, if we take Zen as a religion, Christianity and Zen do seem to be quite different. But their teachings have as their interchange a common area which belongs to both. That is the area of religious experience. I'm sure that a lot of words and phrases in the Bible can never be uttered outside a true religious experience. That it seems to me, is not irrelevant to the satori experience in Zen.

Now, it is of utmost importance for beginners in Zen to comprehend its aims clearly. What are we going to attain by doing zazen? There are three categories:

1. Developing concentration of the mind.
2. Satori-awakening, enlightenment.
3. Personalization of satori.

The first, to develop concentration is of utmost importance in establishing and maintaining a successful life in this world. The ability to concentrate calms the surface of our consciousness. This is most necessary in making correct decisions, and for receiving external impressions and information the right way. Also, when the mind is deeply absorbed, it does not easily yield to the influence of external circumstances. And, moreover, when we want to actualize ideas which arise in our heart, or when we want to accomplish some work or business, a strong concentration of mind is indispensable.

The second, satori, is the most important to a Mahayana Zen Buddhist. Dogen Zenji, the great Zen master who brought Sôtô Zen to Japan, has clearly stated that without enlightenment there is no Zen. This satori does not happen necessarily by mere concentration. This is especially true, if the mind is brought to one-pointedness in the objective world. And even if this is achieved inwardly our life problem, the problem of life and death, cannot be solved fundamentally by concentration. It can only be resolved by enlightenment and the personalization that experience. So if we want to free ourselves from the anxiety of the sufferings of life through zazen, the satori experience should be our main purpose for practicing zazen. Dogen Zenji has told us that we should pray for the help of Buddhas and Patriarchs. This resembles Christianity's prayers of intercession.

The third aim of zazen, the personalization or embodiment of satori, comes as a matter of course only after having attained satori. To attain this experience of enlightenment is not very difficult. For some people, only one sesshin is necessary. But to accomplish our ultimate personality is very difficult indeed, and requires an extremely long period of time. The experience itself is only the entrance. The completion is to personalize what we came to realize in the experience. After washing away all the ecstasy and glitter in the experience, the truly great Zen person is not distinguishable in outward appearance. He is a man who has experienced deep enlightenment and consequently extinguished all illusions, but is still not different externally from an ordinary man. Through satori and zazen, you should not become a strange person, not an eccentric or an esoteric person. You should become a normal person, a real person, and as far as possible, a perfect human being. I think the truly great Christian is not much different!

- by Yamada Kôun

(This talk was given by Yamada Rôshi
on May 9, 1975, at San-Un Zendô
in Kamakura, Japan)

16 The Face of Zen in America?

Zen to Go

Zen Buddhism has been a presence in America since the turn of the century (for a detailed history, see Rick Field's *How the Swans Came to the Lake: the History of Buddhism in America*). Zen Buddhism began to first awaken the intellectual mind of America with the writings of D.T. Suzuki. As Zen Buddhist thought became available, poets, artists, writers, theologians and psychologists became fascinated by the possibilities presented by Zen. And quite possibly, the first distinctions appeared between "Zen" and "Zen Buddhism."

Aspects of "Zen thought" influenced, was absorbed by, and in turn was re-expressed by the Beat Generation, through the turbulent '60s. More Zen Buddhist writings became available, and Americans, such as Alan Watts and Thomas Merton, began writing about Zen. Zen Buddhist teachers began arriving from Asia, and Zen Buddhist monasteries and teaching centers were established that continue to this day.

The term "Zen" has even reached a vague and general sense of familiarity in our culture. At least, the word "Zen" has formed a focus point for such diverse book topics as tennis, computer art, skiing, driving, motorcycle maintenance, writing and Internet surfing. Comedians make references to Zen in the context of paradox, absurd, arcane or incomprehensible subjects. Other references or jokes about Zen have appeared in comic strips ("Zen Pizza? It's one with everything"), a Zen version of *Where's Waldo*, (showing Waldo in meditation, lost not in typical crowds of people, but sitting serenely in vast emptiness, with only the company of a few rocks, a bird, and a bonsai), and some of the cartoons of Gahan Wilson. Musicians have referenced Zen in titles of jazz, rock, and alternative albums (*Music for Zen Meditation*; *Catch Bull at Four*; *Zen Arcade*; *Now and Zen*). *Zazen*, *Zen* and *Zen Buddhism* can be found as references in some collegiate dictionaries.

But for many people, "Zen" is still associated with the exotic and the absurd; almost everyone has at least heard of "the sound of one hand clapping," without the vaguest notion of kôan study. When people learn that you engage in hours of "sitting still, doing nothing," if you are fortunate, you are associated with the exotic. Otherwise, well, you are just plain *weird*. This does not make for good cocktail conversation.

Given that Zen monastic settings do exist in America, most of us do not engage our spiritual search or practice in a monastic setting, either Christian or Buddhist. The cloistered life is simply not a viable option in our contemporary culture. We seek a spiritual practice and rule of life that includes corporate work or entrepreneurship, marriage and family. A practice that is a day to day, moment to moment expression of life: cooking dinner, taking the garbage out, changing the cat litter. Grounded in the reality of the present. This can be a very hard but useful practice; real life quickly tarnishes the false sheen of idealized spirituality and romanticized practice.

This is where a Zen practice, that is not necessarily Buddhist, comes in. And perhaps, this is only conceivable in America.

The challenge, then, is to develop a distinctively, Western, non-monastic lay Zen practice, a practice that emphasizes everyday life in its entirety, as a householder or corporate worker. Is the non-monastic Zen practice of an American in the everyday workaday world "true" Zen practice? Or is this type of Zen merely another expression of the Western preoccupation with fads and trends, destined to become just another "buzz" or self-help program?

The future of Zen in America will be shaped in part by our culture, but more importantly, by individuals who practice. These are questions for all who practice Zen, in any form or tradition.

A fundamental consideration is the viable transmission of the Dharma, the core of which is the experience of enlightenment and the subsequent post-enlightenment refinement.

Padmasambhava, the Eighth century saint who introduced
Buddhism to Tibet, is credited with the following
prophecy:

> When the steel birds fill the sky,
> and iron horses run on rails,
> then the peoples of Tibet
> will be scattered to the wind,
> and the Dharma
> will be reborn
> in the land of the red man.

The "land of the red man" has been interpreted to mean
North America. Is the Dharma actually in rebirth in the
"land of the red man"? Certainly, Tibetan Buddhism has
taken some root in America and the West.

Perhaps the Dharma is awakening in America in the
broadest sense. America is an unparalleled experiment
on the face of the planet, a nation of a frightening mixture
of power, arrogance, benevolence, inventiveness, waste
and consumption.

And yet a nation like no other; a culture made up of
cultures, with no great regard for the past and little vision
for the future, but with incredible potential, with exciting
challenges and opportunities for transformation and
healing, for ourselves and the planet. The likely birthplace
of a new culture that can embrace all cultures, celebrating
both diversity and difference. As a nation, we are slowly
remembering errors of the past, and of the possibilities of
redeeming the future, by awakening to the present.

This awakening is from individual to individual, rippling and radiating out into the culture. As we take absolute and full responsibility for our own lives, these values radiate into family, friends, work, society. The world is changed, transformed, one person at a time. Existing "problems" of drugs, crime, poverty and despair will not be solved by politicians or political systems.

The next revolution will not be political in nature; the only real revolution remaining, is that of *consciousness*.

Dharma transmission, the Great Chain of Being, or the Food Chain?

As a vehicle or expression of the Dharma, is Zen taking root in America, or mutating into some unviable form?

This question leads to other questions that would not be asked in Asia: What is the meaning and form of the practice of Zen for those raised in the Judeo/Christian/ Islamic religious traditions?

Conversely, what can Zen, which has been called "the heart of religion" or "the religion before religion", contribute to the Western religious traditions? Is this a form of heresy, or an exploration of contemplative practice that many feel is missing from lay Christianity? Can non theistic Zen exist in a climate and culture of monotheism?

Perhaps, only in the West, can we even ask this question: can Zen practice be separated from Buddhism; that is, can one who is NOT a professing Buddhist, rather one who is an atheist, agnostic or professing monotheist practice "true" Zen? This seems to be an issue of more than passing interest, and far from being resolved.

Can one be a Buddha without being Buddhist? Ask the frogs ("If by sitting, one becomes a Buddha, then all frogs are Buddhas"). Perhaps it is worth contemplating, that the historical Buddha Gautama Sâkyamuni was not a Buddhist (for that matter, Jesus was not a Christian, nor Mohammed a Muslim).

This is fundamental and critical question for a number of us that sit, but are not drawn to monastic practice or inclined to convert to Buddhism: Can the practice of Zen be separated from the religious traditions of Buddhism?

Zen grew out of the experience of Gautama and was shaped in the context of the emerging religion that became Buddhism, as Gautama's teachings were recorded, codified and transmitted. Zen is one form, purporting to be the "heart" or essence of the transmission of Gautama's experience of awakening. But the practice of Zen, as emphasized by Bodhidharma's Four Marks points to a pure practice devoid and independent of all concepts, beliefs or theology:

- A special transmission outside the scriptures
- No dependence on words or letters
- Direct pointing to the mind
- Seeing one's true nature and the awakened (enlightened) state of being

The point of practicing zazen is multi-faceted and paradoxical: an expression of fundamental sanity; the expression of awakening; the acknowledgment that one is already awakened; to embody the truth of our present reality; to be willing to sit in unknowing or not-knowing.

What can it mean to simply sit zazen without any formal religious preferences?

The purpose of sitting, of prayer, meditation, of participation in rituals, observations, and sacraments is to realize, embody, and express one's ultimate nature, one's true self.

Christians, are called to "repent." For many, this is synonymous with doing penance, feeling guilty, or resolving to change our behavior. But true repentance is much deeper and literally demands a fundamental and radical transformation of our being. In the original Greek, the word used is *metanoia*. *Metanoia* literally means a profound turning about, a complete transformation or "conversion" of one's being. How do we embrace or embody this conversion?

Zen of course has undergone cultural transformations along the way. Zen migrated from India into the Taoist and Confucionist culture of China, where it incorporated elements of both religions. Zen took root in China, grew, mature, and bore fruit, then once again, disappeared. Zen then migrated to Japan, Korea, and Vietnam, again assimilating and incorporating cultural and religious elements, but also in turn influencing the native cultural milieu, all the while adapting, yet remaining Zen.

With the relatively recent introduction of Zen to America and the West, for the first time Zen moves beyond the cultures in which it was born, grew and matured. This is truly a close and alien encounter for our culture, ourselves, and even for Zen itself. Zen must make a difficult transition; remaining truly Zen, becoming truly American.

Perhaps, for the first time ever, Zen will undergo a completely radical transformation, transcending the bounds of Buddhism, to something that is Zen but not Zen, something totally new and as yet unseen. Perhaps the vitality of Zen will take root, will take flame, will burst, consume or transform all constraints of Christianity or Buddhism, of Asian or Western culture, of the Eastern or Western mind set. This is possible, if Zen is indeed "the heart of all religion" or "the religion before religion." Perhaps Zen is like the lightning that flashes from East to West in the clear and empty sky...

There are many who are drawn to Zen from an inexpressible longing in the depths of their being that traditional religions do not speak to. These people come from a variety of religious traditions, and their Zen may take the shape of a distinct exploration of the possibilities of Christian Zen (Zen Baptists, Episcopalians, Catholics?). Others may prefer to take the precepts and become practicing lay or even monastic Buddhists. And others may prefer simply to sit, unconcerned about either the orthodoxy or theology of their practice, from either the Zen or Christian viewpoint.

In this regard, all who practice Zen, in any form, are shaping the face of Zen in America. And all share in the responsibility of the embodiment and transmission of the Dharma, of the Way, the Truth, and the Light.

We continue to sit zazen, beyond the limitations of words, concepts, theologies, categorizations. Just here, just now, breathing in, breathing out; who breathes, you or the universe? Is there any difference between you breathing in the universe, or the universe breathing in you? There is only the breathing.

What then will be the face of Zen in America? As America itself, there will be many faces, and no face. Look in the mirror and see that face. Look in the zendô and behold your face. Look at Tibetan thangkas, at the Buddhas with multiple faces and manifestations: Avalokitésvara, Manjushri, Samantabhadra. Look at stained glass, the crucifix, Orthodox icons.

Perhaps the face is not important; in sitting, the sitting takes care of itself, and these issues become superfluous. The face of no-face?

> staring at the wall,
> staring into space —
> what matters the direction,
> if one has no face?

I am grateful to Yamada Kôun Rôshi, Yasutani Rôshi, Ruben Habito and all the teachers in the Sanbô Kyôdan, to allow the full exploration and expression of the practice of Zen. There is in the practice of zazen a deep sense of homecoming, of belonging or being a part of something that cannot be named, of something beyond traditional forms or labels. There is a complete welcoming and openness to a multitude of expressions, an invitation of freedom to just "be" in a community, without the imposition of any preconditions.

There is the invitation and responsibility to develop my practice and my life, to truly become an "artist of life." I have been fortunate in my journey to encounter individuals from many traditions that have actively encouraged and supported my personal explorations, to have the opportunity to practice Zen under the direction of an authorized teacher, within a unique tradition that may change what is meant by tradition.

As we practice Zen, Zen will change our life. And, our practice will change the life and the face of Zen.

by Rex Robertson

Appendix:　　Mindful Resources

The Three Treasures

- The Buddha
- The Dharma
- The Sangha

The Four Noble Truths

- The truth of the experience of phenomenal existence as unsatisfactory (Sanskrit, *dukkha*, dysfunction)
- The truth of the origin of unsatisfactoriness (Sanskrit, *trishnâ*, desire or craving)
- The truth of the end of unsatisfactoriness (Sanskrit, *nirvâna*, extinguishing the fire)
- The truth of the way to ending unsatisfactoriness (Sanskrit, *mârga*, path; the Eightfold Path)

The Four Vows of the Bodhisattva

- Sentient beings are numberless; I vow to free them
- Delusions are inexhaustible; I vow to end them
- The Dharma gates are boundless; I vow to open them
- The enlightened way is unsurpassable; I vow to embody it

The Four Marks of Zen

- No dependence on words or letters
- A special transmission outside the scriptures
- Direct pointing to the human mind and heart
- Seeing into one's true nature

The Five Central Facts of Buddhism

- I am subject to decay, and I cannot escape it.
- I am subject to disease, and I cannot escape it.
- I am subject to death, and I cannot escape it.
- There will be separation from all that I love
- I am the owner of my deeds. Whatever deed I do, good or bad, I shall become heir to it.

The Eightfold Path

- Right view
- Right thought
- Right speech
- Right action
- Right livelihood
- Right effort
- Right mindfulness
- Right samadhi

The Ten Grave Precepts

- Do not kill
- Do not steal
- Do not be greedy

- Do not tell a lie
- Do not be ignorant
- Do not talk about others' faults
- Do not elevate yourself by criticizing others
- Do not be stingy
- Do not get angry
- Do not speak ill of the Three Treasures

Hakuin's Song of Zazen

From the beginning all beings are Buddha.
Like water and ice, without water no ice, outside us
     no Buddhas.
How near the truth, yet how far we seek.
Like one in water crying, "I thirst!"
Like the son of a rich man wand'ring poor on this
     earth we endlessly circle the six worlds.
The cause of our sorrow is ego delusion.
From dark path to dark path we've wandered in
     darkness, how can we be freed from the
     wheel of samsara?
The gateway to freedom is zazen Samadhi.
Beyond exaltation, beyond all our praises the pure
     Mahayana.
Observing the Precepts, Repentance and Giving,
     the countless good deeds and the Way of
     Right Living, all come from zazen.
Thus one true Samadhi extinguishes evils. It purifies
     karma, dissolving obstructions.
Then where are the dark paths to lead us astray? The

Pure Lotus Land is not far away.
Hearing this truth, heart humble and grateful. To
    praise and embrace it, to practice its Wisdom,
    brings unending blessings, brings mountains
    of merit.
And if we turn inward and prove our True Nature,
    that True Self is no-self, our own self is no-
    self, we go beyond ego and past clever words.
Then the gate to the oneness of cause-and-effect is
    thrown open.
Not two and not three, straight ahead runs the Way.
Our form now being no-form, in going and returning
    never leave home.
Our thought now being no-thought, our dancing and
    songs are the Voice of the Dharma.
How vast is the heaven of boundless Samadhi!
How bright and transparent the moonlight of wisdom!
What is there outside us? What is there we lack?
Nirvana is openly shown to our eyes.
This earth where we stand is the pure lotus land! And
    this very body, the body of Buddha.

The Heart Sûtra

(The Heart of the Perfection of Great Wisdom Sutra)

Avalokitésvara Bodhisattva doing deep Prajna Paramita
    perceived the emptiness of all five conditions,
    and was freed of pain.
O Sariputra, form is no other than emptiness,
    emptiness no other than form;

form is precisely emptiness,
sensation, perception,
reaction and consciousness are also like this.
O Sariputra, all things are expressions of emptiness,
    not born, not destroyed, not stained, not pure;
    neither waxing, nor waning.
Thus emptiness is not form;
    not sensation nor perception,
    reaction nor consciousness;
    no eye, ear, nose, tongue, body, mind;
    no color, sound, smell, taste, touch, thing;
    no realm of sight, no realm of consciousness;
    no ignorance, no end to ignorance;
    no old age and death,
    no cessation of old age and death;
    no suffering, no cause or end to suffering,
    no path, no wisdom and no gain.
No gain - thus Bodhisattvas like this Prajna Paramita
    with no hindrance of mind -
    no hindrance therefore no fear.
Far beyond all such delusion, Nirvana is already here.
All past, present and future Buddhas
    live this Prajna Paramita
    and attain supreme, perfect enlightenment.
Therefore know that Prajna Paramita
    is the holy mantra, the luminous mantra,
    the supreme mantra, the incomparable mantra
    by which all suffering is cleared.
This is no other than truth.

Therefore know that Prajna Paramita
> is the holy mantra, the luminous mantra,
> the supreme mantra, the incomparable mantra
> by which all suffering is cleared.

This is no other than truth.
Therefore set forth the Prajna Paramita mantra,
> set forth this mantra and proclaim:
> Gate Gate Paragate Parasamgate, Bodhi Svaha!

HARADA-YASUTANI LINEAGE

The Sanbo Kyodan is part of a wider Zen community known as the Harada-Yasutani lineage. The latter includes over 90 teachers in Japan, the Philippines, North America and Europe. The following lists some dharma teachers known for their zendos or authorship, who derive their teaching from this wider stream.

- Aitken, Robert Chotan Gyoun Roshi
- Bays, Jan Chozen Soule
- Beck, Charlotte Joko
- Enomiya-Lassalle, Hugo Makibi Aiun-ken
- Glassman, Bernard Tetsugen
- Habito, Ruben
- Harada, Exinn Sogaku
- Hixon, Lex Jikai
- Kapleau, Philip
- Kennedy, Robert Jinsen S.J.Roshi
- Loori, John Daido
- Low, Albert
- Maezumi, Taizan Hakuyu
- Mathiessen, Peter Muryo Roshi

- Merzel, Dennis Genpo Roshi
- Packer, Toni
- Tarrant, John Nanryu Ji`un-ken Roshi
- Yamada, Kôun Zenshin
- Yasutani, Hakuun Ryoko

Webpage Addresses:

- Maria Kannon Zen Center, http://www.mkzc.org/

- Harada-Yasutani School of Zen Buddhism, http://www. ciolek.com/WWWVLPages/ZenPages/ Harada Yasutani.html
  (maintained by Dr. T. Matthew Ciolek)

List of Books:

The following are recommended for further reading.

Aitken, Robert, *Taking the Path of Zen*
Aitken, Robert, *The Mind of Clover*
Anonymous (various translations), *The Cloud of Unknowing*
Brother Lawrence, *The Practice of the Presence of God*
Callaway, Tucker N. , *Zen Way, Jesus Way*
de Caussade, Jean-Pierre , *The Sacrament of the Present   Moment*
de Chardin, Pierre Teilhard , *The Divine Milieu*
de Chardin, Pierre Teilhard , *The Hymn of the Universe*
Enomiya-LaSalle, Fr. Hugo, *Living in the New Consciousness*

Enomiya-LaSalle, Fr. Hugo, *The Practice of Zen Meditation*
Habito, Ruben, *Total Liberation*
Habito, Ruben, *Healing Breath*
Healy, Kathleen, *Entering the Cave of the Heart: Eastern Ways of Prayer for Western Christians*
Hendricks, Gay, *The Corporate Mystic*
Hunter, Dale, *Zen in the Workplace*
Hunter, Dale, *The Zen of Groups*
Johnston SJ, William, *The Still Point: Reflections on Zen and Christian Mysticism*
Johnston SJ, William, *Christian Zen*
Kadowaki SJ, J.K., *Zen and the Bible: A Priest's Experience*
Keating, Thomas, *Open Mind, Open Heart*
Kennedy, Robert, *Zen Spirit, Christian Spirit*
Matus, Thomas, *Yoga and the Christian Tradition: An Experiment in Faith*
Merton, Thomas, *Mystics and Zen Masters*
Merton, Thomas, *Zen and the Birds of Appetite*
Steindl-Rast, Br. David , *Gratefulness, the Heart of Prayer*
Walker, Susan, (Editor) *Speaking of Silence*

Sanbô Kyôdan Lineage from the Buddha

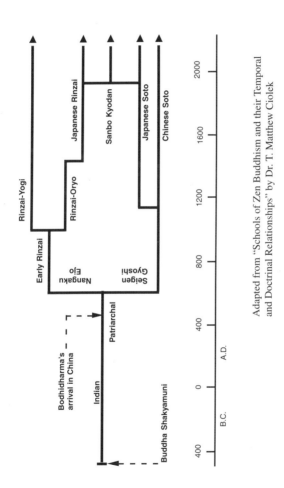

Adapted from "Schools of Zen Buddhism and their Temporal and Doctrinal Relationships" by Dr. T. Matthew Ciolek